Tracking
Wounded
Deer

Tracking Wounded Deer

How to Find and Tag Deer Shot with Bow or Gun

Richard P. Smith

Smith Publications

Tracking Wounded Deer
How to Find and Tag Deer Shot with Bow or Gun

by Richard P. Smith

Published by:
> **Smith Publications**
> Lucy & Richard Smith
> 814 Clark St.
> Marquette, MI 49855

Copyright © 1996 by Richard P. Smith
Second Edition
First Printing 1996
Printed in the United States of America

All photos by the author unless otherwise credited
Cover photo by Richard P. Smith
Cover design by Krone Graphic Design & Lucy Smith
Book production & design by Lucy Smith
Research & Editing by Lucy Smith
Interior layout and design by Kay Richey
Electronically created camera-ready copy by:
> KLR Communications, Inc.
> POB 192
> Grawn, MI 49637
Printed on recycled paper

Library of Congress Cataloging in Publication Data

Smith, Richard P.
Tracking Wounded Deer: How to Find and Tag Deer Shot with Bow or Gun / by Richard P. Smith. - 2nd ed.
1. Deer hunting   2. Tracking and trailing   I. Title
SK301. S67   1996   799.2'77357 SM
ISBN 0-9617407-7-9 Softcover (previously ISBN 0-8117-2265-1)

This book is dedicated to members of

Deer Search, Inc.

and to others who do their utmost to
recover wounded and dead deer

Contents

Acknowledgments

So many people have contributed to this book in some way that I'm bound to forget someone as I jot down these words of thanks. So I will apologize for that up front. Following are the names of some of those who have allowed me to accompany them on a blood trail, shared their stories with me, or helped in some other way.

Sue LaFaive, for example, converted a rough sketch into a professionally done map that will be easy for readers to understand. Charles Alsheimer provided an appropriate photo for one of the chapters. Veterinarians Albert Hollings and Joe Svaboda allowed me to use two important slides showing deer anatomy.

Curt Van Lith took the time to give me a detailed account of how he recovered his record book buck, a story I felt unique enough to deserve a separate chapter. Lengthy interviews with Don and Penny Hickman, John Jeanneney and Hans Klein resulted in another chapter, plus valuable additions to others. Bob McNally put me in touch with Dr. Randy Davidson, who made a valuable contribution to still one more chapter.

Others I would like to thank for their help are Gene Ballew, Jerry Beck, Dave Borgeson, Bob Brandau, Jim Butler, Frank Chapin, John Driver, Bruce and Jason Dupras, Bob Eastman, Mark Eby, George Gardner, Phil Grable, Russ Greenwood, Sam Grissom, Paul Hannuksela, Jim Haveman, Dean Hulce, Maury Jones, Rob Keck, Terry Kemp, Rich LaRocco, George Lovegrove, Gary Marshall, Dan Massee, Dave Raikko, Lennie Rezmer, Dick Rintamaki, Dr. Dave Samuel, Ron Spring, Bob Vincent, Fred Wallace, Bob Wiersma; Dick, Rick and Jim Retaskie.

Last but not least are those others who have shared many hunts with me and tolerated my habit of photographing almost everything. They are my brother Bruce, my uncle George and his son Craig.

I also want to thank Kay Richey for help in reprinting this book. My wife and business partner, Lucy, deserves credit for doing a lot of work on this book; including research, editing, revisions, preparing the deer hair chart and printing the black and white photos.

Introduction

With this book I've attempted to both break new ground and to provide the best information possible on tracking wounded deer. To my knowledge, a set of color photos showing actual blood sign resulting from different types of hits has never been published before. The photos appear here because I think they are essential for showing hunters what they will probably see in the field when they shoot a deer. Also included are closeups of deer hair.

As you will see from these photos, blood sign does not always fit the patterns so often described. There are no absolutes when it comes to tracking wounded deer, and this applies to all aspects of the art, from blood sign to the distances deer travel when shot in certain parts of the body. Every deer is different, and many fail to fit a pattern. There are probably more exceptions than hard and fast rules, a fact I've tried to emphasize throughout the book with specific examples.

The best way to learn anything is through experience, and these pages contain plenty of personal experiences that are sure to benefit you when you face a blood trail of your own. Sooner or later, every deer hunter shoots an animal that runs out of sight before dying and that requires some effort to recover. This book will help prepare you for that time and will increase your chances of recovering that deer and others that may follow.

No hunter likes to wound a deer. We all strive not to. But it sometimes happens, due to the many uncontrollable variables in deer hunting. When it does happen, you should make every effort to find and finish the deer as soon as possible, and this book will help you do that.

Whenever possible, I've used examples from my own personal experiences, either animals I've shot myself or those hit by my hunting companions. As a result, some readers may get the mistaken impression that I or people I hunt with wound a lot of deer. The fact is, most of the deer I and my companions shoot are clean kills. These examples are drawn from more than 30 years of hunting experience, during which time I've shot a lot of deer. Those I've had to follow represent a small sample of my total.

During a recent fall, for example, I tagged five bucks. Two of those deer had to be followed, but one of them barely ran out of sight before dying with a bullet through the heart. The last deer was poorly hit, but I recovered it with no problem by falling back on my years of experience. Those five deer were taken from various states and Canadian provinces. I'm usually fortunate enough to deer hunt in different parts of North America every year.

A better title for this book might be <u>Tracking Wounded and Dead Deer</u> because most of the deer that hunters end up tracking are dead by the time hunters start following them, having simply run out of sight before dying. This is especially true for deer shot by bowhunters.

One more point: although this book deals with tracking deer, much of its information can be applied to all big game, be it bear, elk, moose or whatever. I hope you are spared some of the tracking experiences in this book, but if you aren't, perhaps reading it will help you bring such hunts to a successful conclusion. That's why I wrote it!

1

Hit or Miss?

When you shoot at a mule deer, whitetail, or blacktail with gun or bow, it's usually possible to determine—at the shot—whether you've scored a hit. There will normally be some indication that the bullet, slug, or arrow has connected—but not always. Consider the experience of Maury Jones, with Jackson Hole Country Outfitters in Wyoming.

As a young man in his late teens, Maury was hunting muleys with a .303 caliber British rifle and 180-grain bullets when a buck appeared 50 yards away. He aimed carefully and shot several times at the forkhorn without it showing any sign of being hit. Concerned that he was doing something wrong and the deer would get away, Jones tried aiming both high and low on the animal before emptying the rifle of its seven rounds.

The small buck went out of sight. Maury reloaded and went after it, finding blood where the deer had been. He was relieved and pleased when he found the forkhorn dead after following the blood trail about 150 yards. Amazingly, four of his shots had gone through the buck's chest cavity, though the buck had shown no indication of being hit. That muley wasn't big, either. Maury guessed it weighed no more than 110 pounds dressed.

Part of the reason the deer showed no sign of being hit is that the heavy bullets probably had gone through the chest without much

Even small deer like this forkhorn muley may not show any indication of being fatally hit with a high-powered rifle bullet.

expansion, minimizing shock. If Maury assumed his shots had missed, based on the buck's lack of reaction, and left without checking, he would have walked away from a dead deer. Some hunters unknowingly leave hit deer because they assume they missed.

Maury Jones later put one of his tags on a buck another hunter didn't follow up on. Hunting in Colorado, when there was snow on the ground, he came across the fresh tracks of a group of muleys. One set of prints looked like those of a buck, so he followed. The tracks eventually led to a logging road, where a hunter came along in a vehicle, saw the deer, got out, and took a shot. Apparently, the hunter thought he'd missed, was too lazy to check on the outcome, and so he drove off.

Maury said he thought about leaving the deer's tracks when he came to the logging road, since he figured the shot had spooked the deer, but he decided to go farther. It's a good thing he did. He found blood where the road hunter's bullet had hit the buck, and the forkhorn was dead 100 yards away, shot through the lungs.

Big-game hunting consultant Rich LaRocco from Wellsville, Utah, tells a similar story. He was stalking a mule deer buck for a closer rifle shot when another hunter took a shot at it from a distance of 400 to 450 yards across a canyon. Despite the long range, the shot scored a good hit and took the buck through the lungs. When he saw the buck go down, Rich assumed the shooter knew he'd connected, so he left the carcass where it fell. He checked the site hours later, however, and discovered the deer was still there. By then, the meat was no longer salvageable. The shooter had left without checking for a hit.

On long-distance shots, high-velocity rifle bullets sometimes don't expand as they normally would, especially if no bones are hit. They pass completely through animals without causing much shock. Consequently, a fatally hit deer may not show any sign of being hit. And the greater the distance between hunter and deer, the harder it is to detect any reaction from a hit. Rifle recoil after a shot can distract a hunter long enough that he or she misses an obvious indication of a hit.

Rich LaRocco once guided a deer hunter who was about to take a long shot at a buck. While the guy was preparing to shoot, Rich

Jim Haveman examines antlers from a Wyoming mule deer that went unrecovered, perhaps because the hunter who shot it mistakenly thought he had missed and didn't follow.

watched the deer through binoculars. At the shot, the buck went down immediately. Because of the recoil, however, the hunter failed to see this. He assumed he had missed because the deer was no longer in sight. If Rich hadn't been there to witness what happened, his client might have been unaware of how good a shot he had made and might have left his prize.

Similar situations develop for whitetail and blacktail deer, too, at both close and long range. Michigan hunter Mike Mingori, for exam-

Mike Mingori with the whitetail buck he initially thought he had missed but found the next day.

ple, took a 30-yard shot at a big whitetail buck with a .32 caliber rifle one evening. There was snow on the ground, and the buck ran off at the shot. Mike said the buck stumbled a couple of times as it ran off, but he thought it was simply slipping in the snow. He could find no blood or hair on the snow to confirm a hit, so he assumed he'd missed.

Mike did a lot of thinking about that shot overnight. He couldn't imagine how he'd missed such a close one. Returning to the site the following morning, he followed the buck's tracks. It was dead 50 yards from where it had been standing at the shot. One of the buck's shoulders was broken, but there wasn't a drop of blood.

Fatally hit deer don't always bleed externally, especially when shot with traditional "brush guns" like the .30-30, .32, and .35. And I've seen the same thing on whitetails hit with shotgun slugs, buckshot, or muzzle-loading rifles. In fact, it can happen regardless of the weapon used.

One fall my brother shoulder-shot a six-point whitetail with a .30-30. The buck covered 200 yards before going down. Even though the bullet exited, the buck ran over 150 yards before dropping any blood on the ground. We found hair where the deer had been standing, confirming a hit, but without snow or blood it was impossible to trail the deer. So we conducted a random search in the direction the deer had run and finally we found it.

I once put a 12 gauge shotgun slug into the chest of an eight-point whitetail that ran 140 yards before dropping, and there was no visible blood along his trail for at least the first 75 yards. Fortunately, there was snow, but there were also a lot of deer tracks. It took me a good 30 minutes to sort out the buck's tracks from those of other deer and finally find him. I was starting to have serious doubts about whether I had hit that deer until I eventually found blood.

One time Don Hickman of Pleasant Valley, New York, was using a leashed dog to track a wounded whitetail buck when he came upon a dead doe that had been gut shot.

"Oh, that must be the deer Joe shot at this evening," said one member of the party. "He thought he missed."

The lesson here is this: DEER HUNTERS SHOULD NEVER ASSUME THAT A SHOT MISSED. ALWAYS ASSUME YOU HIT THE ANIMAL UNTIL A THOROUGH SEARCH CONFIRMS OTHERWISE. In regard to long-distance shots, never shoot at a deer farther away than you are willing to walk to check on the shot's outcome.

As the above examples illustrate, hunters must go to the spot where a deer was standing when shot at, and beyond, to accurately determine whether the animal was hit. Hunters who aren't willing to do that shouldn't shoot in the first place. When you're following up on long shots, it is extremely important to accurately mark the location where a deer was standing before you start toward it. Pick prominent landmarks to help guide you to the exact spot; the location will look different once you reach it.

If hunting with a partner, have him or her stay at the place from which you shot and guide you to the exact spot where the deer was standing. While shooting, it's also a good idea for partners to be watching a deer for any reaction to the shot, and to see where your bullets hit if they miss the animal.

In some cases, it's possible to actually hear a bullet striking a deer on a long shot. On a miss, the sound of a bullet striking a tree or the ground might be mistaken for a hit. I recently hunted in Saskatchewan with Proud Foot Creek Outfitters and watched as another hunter fired his .308 at a big buck in a field about 225 yards away. I thought I heard the first shot connect, and the buck whirled around, then stopped broadside again.

At the second shot there was the unmistakable hollow thud of a solid hit, and the buck dropped. I saw the whitetail go down, but the hunter didn't, due to the recoil from his rifle. I thought we would find two holes in the 266-pound, 11-point trophy, but there was just one, from the second shot. Apparently, I was fooled by the sound of the first bullet hitting the ground (there were no trees behind that buck).

Bowhunters are often close enough to deer to both hear and see their arrow connect. But it's not always possible to follow the flight of an arrow, and sounds can be deceiving, too. I took a bow shot at a deer in poor light one time and heard the distinct sound of my broadhead hitting a rock. It was natural to assume I'd missed, but upon checking my arrow, I discovered that the shaft had gone through the deer before hitting the rock.

A solid body hit with an arrow usually produces a muffled thud. If a broadhead hits heavy bone, there will normally be a loud crack. Sometimes an arrow that passes completely through the body or that connects high or low may look like a miss. The eyes can be deceived as well as the ears. Bowhunters who do see their arrow hit a deer and know where it struck have a distinct advantage. Knowing the type of hit is important in determining the next steps.

We've already established that it's not always possible to determine, by a deer's actions alone, whether it has been hit. However, many hit deer exhibit some reaction. An animal may flinch, stumble, shudder, hunch up, drop its tail, jump, kick with its hind legs, or break into a dead run. If a deer runs off after a shot, watch carefully to

Deer like this muley buck may run off after being hit, showing no sign of injury. The movement and momentum of deer that are running when shot at may mask visible signs of injury.

determine if it stumbles, makes a sudden change in direction, or has an unusual gait. A whitetail with a broken leg or shoulder, for example, may limp or favor one side.

A common reaction of whitetails hit solidly with an arrow is to run off at top speed. There have been cases, however, where broadheads passed cleanly through whitetails and muleys, apparently without their knowing they'd been hit. The deer went about their business until suddenly collapsing. On a recent hunt I arrowed a spike whitetail that kicked with its hind legs after being hit. I've seen both whitetails and muleys do this when struck by a bullet.

Whitetails are supposed to clamp their tails down when hit, but this is a less reliable indicator than other reactions—I've seen injured whitetails run off with tails at full mast, and I've seen uninjured whitetails with their tails down. In recent years, I've noticed that more bucks and does keep their tails down when fleeing from people, even when they aren't shot at—apparently to make themselves less visible.

Running deer are less likely to show an immediate visible reaction to being hit than those standing still or walking; their body movements and momentum may mask the reaction.

Carefully watch every deer you shoot at for any clue that you connected, and where. If you don't see or hear a sign of a hit, never assume a miss, as too many other hunters have. Always assume you scored, and do everything possible to recover the deer you shot at, until you are firmly convinced the shot missed.

2

Determining Where You Hit

To confirm a hit on a deer, regardless of the animal's reaction at the shot, look for hair and blood. The quantity and color of hair and blood can also serve as important clues in determining where a deer was hit. Knowing hit location is extremely valuable in deciding how to proceed with the recovery. If neither hair nor blood is immediately visible, that doesn't mean a shot missed, as discussed in chapter 1.

In the vast majority of cases, hair will be present where a deer was standing when hit. Strands of hair can be hard to see at times, and you may have to get down on hands and knees to find them. Hair is easiest to see on snow. Bullets and broadheads knock and cut hair loose as they enter and exit a deer. An exit wound often yields more hair than an entry wound.

The type of hair from an exit wound may also be different than strands from the entry, depending upon the angle of the shot. As you fire, keep in mind a deer's position and which side you shot at; then try to determine if hair you find is from entry or exit. When exiting a deer, bullets, slugs, and arrows often push hair away from the animal, and strands can be found beyond where it was standing. A broadhead that exits a deer frequently contains hair from that part of the body rather than from where it entered.

Hair from different parts of a deer's body varies enough in length,

Craig Smith examines hair from one of his arrows that connected. Deer hairs often show up better on snow than bare ground. By examining them, hunters can often tell where their shot connected.

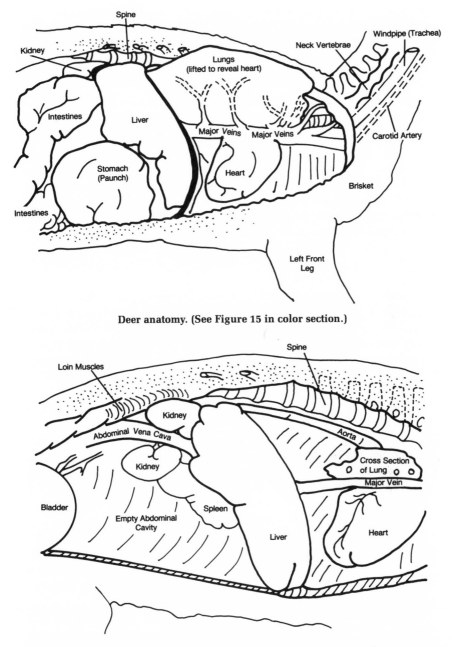

Deer anatomy. (See Figure 15 in color section.)

Deer anatomy—*continued*. (See Figure 16 in color section.) *Drawings courtesy Albert Rollings, DVM and Joe Svaboda, DVM.*

coloration, and structure that it is usually possible to determine from where individual strands came after careful examination. Most deer hairs may appear gray or white on the ground because most of their length is that color. The tips contain most of the differences in color. Whitetail hair will be used here to illustrate these differences, which are very similar on mule and blacktail deer. One difference between mule deer and whitetails is muleys have less white hair on their undersides. Mule deer, however, have a white rump patch that whitetails lack.

Although there are distinct differences in hair from a whitetail's back, belly, chest, and rump, strands from most of the side of the body, from the shoulder back to the flank, are similar. Body hairs are 2½–2¾ inches long and are gray over most of their length. There will be a band of brown or tan near the tip, with black both above and below it. So the tips of these hairs are black, with brown below, black again, and the rest gray. The width of the brown band may vary from one deer to another, and may be widest in the shoulder area, with less black below it than above.

Body hairs may indicate a hit in the lungs, liver, or paunch. Hunters who find this type of hair will have to use other information to determine what type of hit they got. Try to remember where your sights were on the deer at the shot and whether the target was stationary or moving. How did the deer react? Deer struck in the paunch have a tendency to hunch up. A lung or liver hit may make a deer take off at a dead run.

Hairs from the lower side (just above the belly) and from the chest vary from those on the rest of the side. They are black-tipped with brown or tan below, and most of their 2¾–3-inch length is whitish-gray. Longer hairs very similar to those on the lower side are located behind the front leg in the area of the heart. They are 3¾ inches long, with the upper half tan and the lower half whitish-gray. The tips are black. Short, fine, white hairs are found on the inside of the front legs and may be mixed with longer body hairs from a heart shot.

Hairs on the top of a whitetail's back and neck are the darkest, with more than half of their 2½ to 2¾-inch length being black from the tip back. Back hairs from some whitetails have brown bands near the tips; those from others don't. The lower portion of back hairs are gray.

Hairs on top of the neck are colored similarly to those on the back and are about 2½ inches long. Other neck hairs are shorter, about 1½ inches long, and finer. The remainder of the hairs' length is gray like those on the body. Hairs from the outside of the front legs are similar to

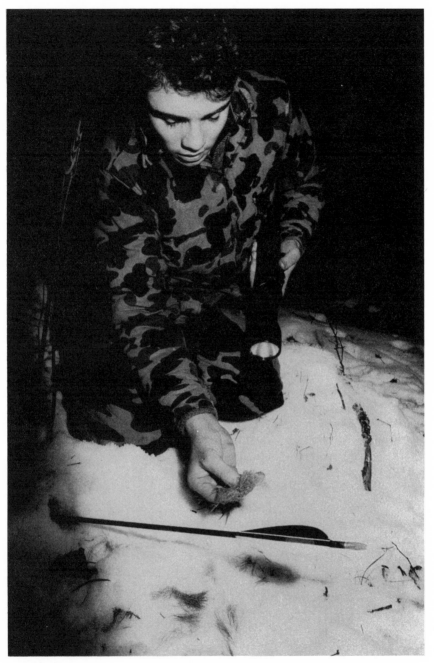
Hunter examines clumps of hair knocked off a deer by an arrow that grazed it.

those from most of the neck, except that the bases may be a little lighter in color. Front leg hairs I've measured were 1 1/2-1 3/4 inches long.

Brisket hairs are coarse and curly, with long black tips. Most of their 2-inch length is whitish-gray. Coarse and curly hairs 2 inches long are also found on the hindquarters or hams. Ham hairs are tipped in black and brown, are gray below and have whitish-gray bases.

White, curly hairs 2-3 inches long are found on the belly. They are hollow like most of the others on a whitetail's body. However, the fine white hairs about 3 1/2 inches long that grow between the hind legs are not hollow. Hairs from the top of the whitetail's tail will be either all black or black-tipped with a wide band of brown, then black again all the way to the base. Long white hairs that measure 4-5 inches are found on the underside of the tail.

In my examination of deer hair, I've noticed variations from one animal to another in different parts of North America. One of the best ways to get a fix on hair is to examine animals you or someone in your party has shot, and compare them to figure 17 in the color section. As a handy reference for illustrating how deer hair varies from different parts of a deer's anatomy, strands of hair can be glued or taped to a piece of cardboard and labeled. For reference in the field, hair can be put in plastic sandwich bags with a piece of paper to label them.

Keep in mind that on most solid hits you will find individual hairs or small clumps on the ground at the spot where your shot connected. If you find large clumps with pieces of skin attached, the bullet or arrow probably grazed the animal. A cousin of mine made such a hit on a recent hunt; passing along the deer's body, his arrow cut off large patches of hair. Snow helped us follow the deer. Since we found no blood we were sure it wasn't hurt.

In another case, my brother gut shot a buck with a black powder rifle. The ball must have grazed part of the deer before entering the body because we found large clumps of hair on the ground. There was blood sign, too, and the buck's actions indicated he was hurt. So we followed and found it. Always triple check for signs of a hit.

If plenty of blood results from shooting a deer, this type of sign can be more important than hair because it provides a way to follow the animal - as long as bleeding continues. The severity and location of a wound can sometimes be determined from blood sign, too. Pink or bright red foamy blood, for example, indicates a lung hit. That's the type most hunters hope to find.

The lungs themselves are generally pink in color. When they are

George Lovegrove compares hair from a deer he shot with samples in plastic to determine where his bullet hit.

damaged, blood filled with small air bubbles is blown out of a deer's nose or mouth as it runs. Often it is sprayed to the sides of the line of travel. But the absence of bubbles in the blood doesn't mean the lungs were missed. My brother recently bow-shot a doe from a ground stand. The arrow hit both lungs and clipped the top of the heart, with the shaft passing completely through the animal. Blood sign was profuse over the 150 yards the deer ran before collapsing, but I didn't notice any typical lung blood. When we reached her, however, her side was covered with foamy red blood from the wound.

Bubbly blood may also result when the windpipe is severed. Dave Borgeson made such a hit on a bowhunt I participated in a number of years ago. Dave's broadhead severed the carotid artery, which hunters commonly call the jugular vein, in addition to the windpipe on a six-point whitetail. There was a heavy, bright red blood trail containing bubbles much larger than those that result from a lung hit. Bright red blood is typical of wounds involving major arteries. The blood trail was a short one—the buck traveled only 60 yards before dropping.

I've also seen a few bubbles in bright red blood that I believe was coughed up by or blown from the nose of arrowed deer. None of those animals was hit in the lungs.

Heart-shot deer also leave a trail of bright red blood. Major blood vessels run the length of the body under the backbone (aortic artery) and on the inside of both hind legs (femoral arteries). The carotid arteries are found on each side of the windpipe in the neck. Two other, smaller arteries carry blood to the stomach (pyloric) and liver (renal-caval) from the heart.

Muscle hits produce bright red blood too, so you may have to evaluate several clues to determine hit location after a shot that produces this type of blood. When major arteries are cut, blood often sprays off to the sides of a deer's trail. A bullet, slug, or arrow that breaks a hind leg may also rupture a femoral artery. The presence of bone fragments often indicates a broken leg. A deer with a broken leg will usually leave three-track patterns rather than four.

It is possible to figure out which leg is broken by carefully examining the tracks to see which print is missing. A couple of characteristics separate prints of front feet from those of rear feet. First of all, the front hooves are larger. In addition, the dew claws are closer to the hooves on front feet than on the rear. If only one front foot print is visible and it's on the left side, the right front leg is broken or injured.

Dark red blood is characteristic of deer hit in the liver or guts. The presence of food particles or intestinal matter, either alone or mixed with blood, is evidence of a paunch or gut shot. Bowhunters who retrieve their arrows after gut-shooting a deer can invariably determine the location of their hit by examining and smelling the shaft. Arrows that pass through the stomach will often hold coarse food particles; those that pierce the intestines will contain a green slimy substance. A strong odor clings to arrows that have gone through stomach or intestines. Little or no blood may be visible on such an arrow.

Blood sign on arrows can also tell you the amount of penetration achieved. Lots of blood over much of the shaft is obviously a good sign. If only one or two of the feathers or vanes have blood on them, the shaft may have simply grazed the animal rather than making a solid hit. The same thing is probably true if only one side of the arrow contains blood. Arrows covered with tallow and little blood are characteristic of hits high in the back and in the brisket.

However, even grazing hits that sever the Achilles tendon or slice open the belly can prove fatal. Examples of each can be found in following chapters.

Bowhunters who hear a loud crack when their arrow hits a deer, and see that the shaft gets little penetration, probably hit the shoulder blade. The more penetration, the better; however, a broadhead needn't go all the way through a deer's body to kill it. An animal can be brought down with as little as a few inches of penetration. Again— always follow a deer you've hit as far as possible.

Blood sign can sometimes fool you. It may not always reveal the full extent of a deer's injuries. A bullet or broadhead may puncture both liver and lungs or liver and stomach, depending upon the deer's stance in relation to you at the time of the shot.

On a recent hunt out of Callaway Gardens near Columbus, Georgia, for instance, fellow writer Jerry Almy took an angling-away shot at a nine-point buck with his .30-06, and it ran out of sight after being hit. Based on the blood trail, it looked as if the buck had been hit in the stomach and liver. There was dark red blood containing coarse food particles. Jerry's bullet did indeed penetrate the stomach and liver, but it continued forward, also taking out the lungs. The deer covered only about 80 yards before collapsing.

Try to consider all factors in figuring where you've hit a deer. It may make a difference in recovery of the animal. Refer to the color section in this book to see what blood sign from different types of hits look like.

3

Blood Trailing Basics

Following the blood trail of a wounded deer can be a simple matter—as long as you are not color blind, there's a steady flow of blood, the trail is in a relatively straight line, and it doesn't go far. If you're color blind, hunt with someone who isn't or arrange for acquaintances who can be called on for help if a hit deer runs out of sight. Color-blind bowhunters can rely on string trackers as an aid in recovering deer. These devices are covered in detail in a later chapter.

I would hazard a guess that a good blood trail results from 50 to 75 percent of properly placed shots. In most other cases, there will be a fair to poor blood trail, or sometimes none. This book is geared toward helping hunters find those deer that leave fair, poor, and no blood trails—even if the animals aren't hit properly. Proper shot placement generally means hits through the lungs and/or heart. But the term can be expanded to include those that break the neck or spine or hit any other vital spot that drops a deer and renders it immediately recoverable—even though the hunter may not have been aiming for those points.

Whenever you shoot at a deer, it's important to notice and remember as many details as possible while the animal is in sight, which may be only seconds. Be especially mindful of the deer's location, its reaction to the shot, where the animal goes out of sight, and its direc-

Always try to remember where a deer was standing when you shot, as well as where you were standing at the time.

tion of travel. After the deer is out of sight, listen for any clues that might help you determine its route or actions, and at the same time, visually mark the location where the deer left the scene.

Pick a prominent landmark that you can use for later reference. You may even want to take a compass reading on the deer's last-known location based on what you heard. Before leaving the spot you shot from, look for a landmark, such as a tree or bush, where the deer was when you shot. If the shot was taken from a position that will not be easy to find again, it is a good idea to leave a marker there too. Any brightly colored item—like a backpack, hat, vest, or coat—makes a good marker. If you have surveyor's tape, white tissue paper, or a spool of Game Tracker line, those can be used too.

This precaution may seem like a lot of bother, but it doesn't really take long and can prove valuable later when you try to piece together what happened. With experience, you'll find that looking after these details becomes automatic.

Telltale sounds that can be helpful are those of the animal falling and then gasping for breath or making gurgling noises. You are in luck if you hear them, because they mean your shot got the lungs. If the disturbance made by a fleeing deer ends abruptly, it may have fallen, lain down, stopped, slowed to a walk, or reached quiet ground.

Hunters who hear their deer go down and die can proceed directly to the animal by heading toward the last sounds. If you're unsure exactly where it went down, try to intersect the course it was on before it fell; look for blood and the animal's tracks. If the outcome of the shot is in doubt, gun hunters should go to where they saw the deer last and try to find a blood trail to confirm a hit, then follow it. If you are using a single-shot firearm, be sure to reload first.

It is generally better for bowhunters to wait a while before following up on their shots, but there are a number of exceptions. If, for example, it is raining or snowing and loss of the blood trail is possible, an archer should follow any blood right away. In dry, arid areas, blood sign can disappear quickly through evaporation and soaking into the soil. Follow quickly in this type of terrain, especially when temperatures are high. When there's good snow cover, bowhunters can follow an arrowed deer soon after it's hit because the animal can still be tracked if it's jumped prematurely. However, it is still advisable to wait in many cases. In open terrain where visibility is good, both bow and gun hunters should immediately follow after a wounded deer that disappears from view, in an effort to keep it in sight and monitor its progress.

Another reason to wait before taking up the trail of a wounded deer, unless you are sure of a quick kill, is that pushing such an animal in an area crawling with hunters increases chances that the animal will walk or run in front of someone else. Frankly, I cannot understand why anyone would deer hunt under those circumstances anyway. I have not hunted where I'd have to be concerned about someone else tagging a deer I shot, and I hope I never do.

Whenever you are following a wounded deer, proceed cautiously and as quietly as possible in order to spot the animal before it spots you and to avoid alarming it. If it's still alive and you get the jump on it, try to get another shot. If another shot isn't possible, watch the deer to determine the extent of its injuries. If it's bedded, it may be best to leave quietly and return later. If you choose that option, though, make sure you'll be able to find that spot again.

Bowhunters who decide to wait before following up can stay at the spot of the shot or leave the area as quietly as possible to avoid spooking animals that may have bedded nearby. Later chapters discuss how long to wait before starting to track deer, based on where they are hit. These suggested waiting periods are not hard and fast rules, but simply guidelines.

Fig. 1 *(right)*. Dark red blood from the liver. Dark blood with stomach contents or intestinal matter mixed in is typical of a gut shot.

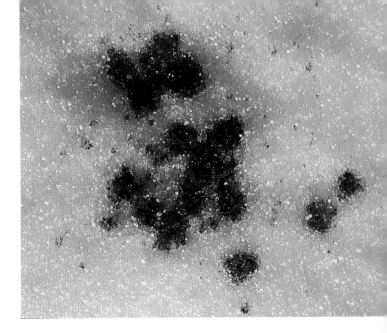

Fig. 2. Two lines of blood side by side indicate that the bullet, slug, or arrow made an exit wound and that both entry and exit holes are bleeding. The bright red blood shown here is typical of a muscle wound. The deer that left this blood trail was gut-shot, but no stomach or intestinal matter was visible.

Fig. 3 *(below)*. The bed of a gut-shot deer, with blood at the rear. The presence of droppings helps determine where the rear portion of the bed is. Blood originated from bleeding muscles rather than an internal injury.

Fig. 4 *(left)*. An accumulation of blood forms where a wounded deer stops and stands for a while.

Fig. 5 *(below)*. Pink, foamy blood in the nostril of a lung-shot deer. As the deer runs, this type of blood is blown from its nose and mouth and may be seen along the trail.

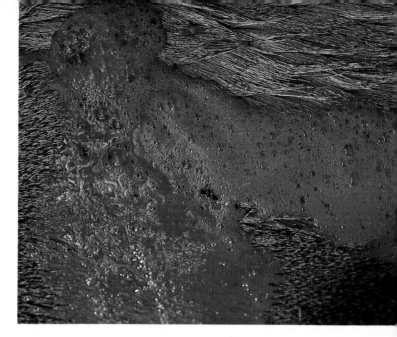

Fig. 6 *(right)*. Bright red, bubbly blood from a lung wound. Lung blood is not always pink.

Fig. 7. Dark red blood like this is often associated with a liver or gut shot. However, the deer that left this profuse blood trail was shot through the heart and lungs.

Fig. 8. Blood may change color when it freezes. This pink-looking blood was left by a deer with a broken front leg, meaning a muscle wound, not a lung hit.

Fig. 9. Pieces of bone are a sure sign of a broken leg.

Fig. 10 *(left)*. **Blood often splatters in the direction a deer was moving. Splatter marks or fingers of blood can point you in the right direction.**

Fig. 11 *(right)*. Look for smears of blood above the ground as well as on it, as shown here. This deer was hit high in the body, and the aortic artery was cut, but so was the stomach. Blood smears usually indicate how high a deer was hit.

Fig. 12 *(left)*. Arrow recovered from a gut shot. Both intestinal and stomach contents are on the shaft.

Fig. 13 *(above)*. Rust spots like the one on this leaf look like blood. They can also be seen on pine needles. To tell the difference, wet a finger and try to wipe the spot off. If it comes off, it's usually blood.

Fig. 14 *(left)*. If a blood trail is snowed on, blood will soak to the surface of the snow when the spot is stepped on. Blood spots are visible in a person's footprint here.

Fig. 15. Internal organs of a deer. (See line drawing on page 23.) *Photo by Albert Rollings, DVM and Joe Svaboda, DVM.*

Fig. 16. Another view of the positioning of internal organs. (See line drawing on page 23.) *Photo by Albert Rollings, DVM and Joe Svaboda, DVM.*

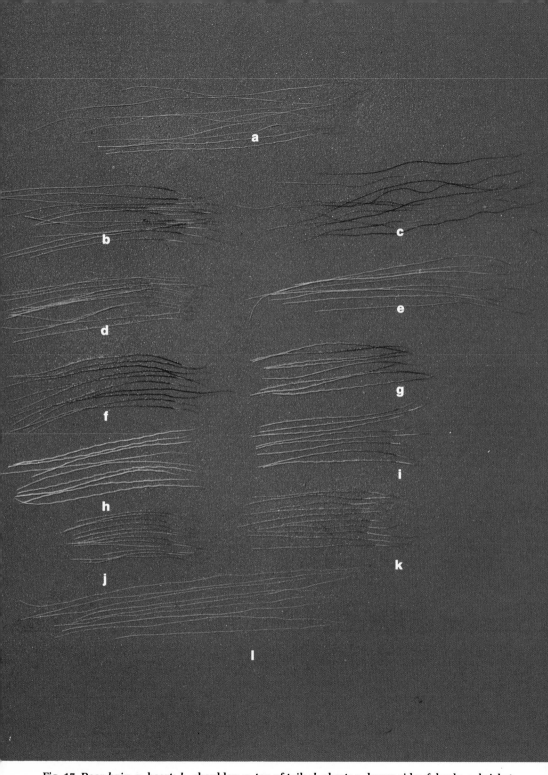

Fig. 17. *Deer hair: a*, heart; *b*, shoulder; *c*, top of tail; *d*, chest; *e*, lower side; *f*, back; *g*, brisket; *h*, belly; *i*, ham; *j*, outside front leg; *k*, neck; and *l*, between hind legs.

There's been some healthy debate in recent years about waiting versus not waiting. As a general rule of thumb, based on lots of experience, I feel it is best for bowhunters to wait and for those using firearms to track a hit deer as soon as possible. There are exceptions, however, and they will be discussed throughout this book. At times, gun hunters should wait and bowhunters shouldn't. The best choice usually depends on the individual circumstances. To say that either waiting or not waiting is always the best policy before starting after an injured deer is an attempt to simplify something that is beyond simplification.

Regardless of what you are hunting with, the philosophy of waiting versus not waiting before trailing a deer boils down to this: sometimes either may be appropriate, but one option may be better than the other. In many cases when deer are recovered, they may be tagged regardless of which option a hunter chooses. It takes experience to determine which is best, and there are times when both approaches can be used. A hunter may start following a deer right away, but then he might back off and wait if the whitetail, blacktail, or muley is jumped without an opportunity for another shot and there is danger of losing the trail if the deer is pushed.

Some hunters who wait and then don't recover a wounded deer blame the delayed action. The only circumstance in which I can envision laying the blame there is if another hunter tags the deer before the original hunter arrives—and that may happen anyway under crowded conditions, whether or not the deer is followed immediately. A delay in tracking a hit deer does not result in loss of the deer. A poor hit does. A poor hit remains a poor hit whether a deer is followed within seconds or hours. This also holds true for fatal hits.

When an injury is not immediately fatal to a deer, you should wait before following. A deer that's going to die within 15 minutes, for example, can cover a lot of ground within that time if pushed immediately—unless a hunter can shoot it again, which gun hunters have a much better chance of doing than bowhunters. If another shot is not possible or is missed, that deer can go far enough to complicate recovery. The farther a deer travels from where it's hit, the greater are the chances that bleeding will stop or the deer will pull a maneuver that the hunter will have a hard time unraveling.

Most fatally hit deer, if not disturbed, won't travel any farther than absolutely necessary before slowing to a walk and stopping. Refraining from pushing them reduces the distance they cover before dying and increases your chances of finding them. Fatally hit deer die whether or not they are pushed. Even if it takes slightly longer for a bedded deer to die than one on its feet, it is still to the hunter's advantage that the animal not go any farther than necessary before succumbing. Based on my experience with hundreds of deer, that travel distance is shortest when the hunter waits before following.

With that out of the way, let's discuss how to follow a blood trail. You've already waited as long as you thought necessary, and have found the beginning of a blood trail, either where you last saw the deer or between there and where the deer was hit. Keep in mind that depth perception can fool—the animal may actually have been closer or farther away from you than it appeared. With this in mind, start look-

Tissue paper is great for marking blood sign because it is easy to see and is biodegradable.

Brightly colored surveyor's tape, such as Jim Haveman is tying to a tree, can also be used to mark a blood trail.

ing for blood sooner than you may think you have to and continue looking beyond where you assume the deer was standing.

Start marking the blood trail as soon as you find it—unless there's snow or a steady line of plentiful blood. If, however, the snow is melting and you don't expect it to last long, it's better to mark the line. You'll also want to start marking blood sign when the trail tapers off, with fewer blood spots and increased distance between them.

Tissue paper or brightly colored surveyor's tape are old standbys for marking blood trails. Now I tend to use spools of Game Tracker line, primarily when hunting with firearms. When I'm bowhunting, I usually have the line attached to my arrow in the first place. If the

string on my arrow breaks before a deer goes down, though, I find the
end and then start pulling line from the spool on my bow and trail it
behind me. There are advantages to marking a blood trail with a continuous line rather than with spaced markers, and it's easier to un-
spool line than it is to stop at intervals and place pieces of tissue or
tape where they will be visible. Both surveyor's tape and tracking line
must be picked up before you leave the woods with your deer.

Teaming up with at least one partner can be a more effective way
of following a blood trail than going it alone. One person can mark the
trail as the others look for blood. If only two people are working
together, both can look for blood sign if the trail is hard to follow, as
long as each new spot or smear is clearly marked before you continue
forward. Two or three hunters are ideal for following a blood trail, and
four aren't bad as long as they are organized and work together as a
team. One of the biggest advantages of working a blood trail with
companions is that you tend to keep each other motivated, persisting
longer than a single hunter normally would alone.

If more than four people are attempting to follow a blood trail,
those with the least amount of experience should simply observe or
mark blood sign, unless asked to do otherwise. Either the person who
shot the deer or the hunter with the most experience should take
charge and keep everyone organized. Inexperienced searchers who go
off on their own can unknowingly overlook or eliminate important
sign. It's also important to keep noise to a minimum—another reason
the number of trackers should be kept to a minimum. Hand signals
should be used to communicate whenever possible. Any talking
should be done in whispers.

Remaining quiet reduces the chances of spooking the quarry, and
makes it easier to hear an injured deer that gets up and moves.

When drops of blood from a wounded deer fall to the ground,
they often splatter. These splatter marks or fingers of blood tend to
point in the direction the deer was traveling. When a deer is stationary,
drops of blood tend to splatter in all directions. Such bits of information can tell you not only when and which way a deer is moving but
also when a deer doubles back or circles. Hunters are most likely to
lose a blood trail where a deer makes a sudden change in direction.

Sometimes you have to track wounded deer after dark, and waiting until full dark or even the middle of the night is often far better
than following the deer too soon. A Coleman-type lantern is best for
blood trailing because it throws a lot of light, but large flashlights will
do. If you're miles from a road, home, or camp, a small flashlight may
have to do because that's what you're likely to have with you.

A lantern is best for blood-trailing after dark.

Always carry spare bulbs and batteries on remote deer hunts. Rich LaRocco, who does a lot of mule deer hunting in remote terrain in the West, always carries two flashlights, plus spare bulbs and three spare sets of batteries for each light. There have been times when he has had to use all of his backup batteries and bulbs.

Night trailing is especially important when the weather is warm or hot, to prevent spoilage of meat. A dead deer should be field-dressed as soon as possible to allow the carcass to cool. Night tracking is also important if rain or snow is expected before morning, and in locations where coyotes and bears have a habit of claiming wounded deer.

If getting a dressed deer out of the woods after dark is a problem, either hang it or prop it open so it cools, and mark the spot carefully so you can relocate it. Leaving a garment with the carcass will often keep coyotes and bears away. If a carcass is on the ground, make sure it is screened from above to keep ravens and vultures away from the meat.

Carefully marking a blood trail at night serves a double purpose: it helps lead you to the deer, and it creates a line of markers you can easily follow back to the starting point.

If snow unexpectedly covers a blood trail, don't give up hope. By walking on snow along the course a deer took, it is sometimes possible to locate blood. Blood will soak through snow that has been stepped on. Dogs with good noses can smell blood under the snow. Chapter 14 deals with the use of dogs to locate dead and wounded deer.

When blood trailing a deer, I use each spot of blood I find as a pivot point for finding the next. I put one foot next to the blood I've located. Then I lean or take a half step in the direction I think the deer is going, and I look ahead and to the sides as far as possible for another spot of red. I also scan standing vegetation such as ferns, bushes,

Look for blood sign on leaves, brush, and trees above ground level as well as on the ground. Sometimes most of the blood will be smeared above the ground.

saplings, and tree branches and trunks. In some cases, most blood sign appears above ground level rather than on the ground.

An experienced bowhunter in New York State phoned Don Hickman one night to ask him for help locating a deer he'd hit. The arrow had struck the buck high in the back, but the hunter couldn't find any blood. It was after dark, so Don used a light. He had walked, bent over, only 20 to 30 yards from where the whitetail was hit, when his eye caught red on brush four feet off the ground. He said it looked like a spray can had been used to paint the brush red. The broadhead had apparently cut the aortic artery, and there was a steady spray of red on the brush along the buck's path, which led only 100 yards. The bowhunter had concentrated his search for blood on the ground, entirely missing the obvious sign above it.

If I don't find any new blood in the direction I think the deer should have gone, I search to the right and then left, usually moving my leading foot in those directions but keeping my other foot near last blood. Once I do see more blood, I move to that spot and repeat the process. By holding in my hand a spool of Game Tracker line that unravels as I move, or having someone else mark blood, I'm not distracted and can concentrate on following the trail as fast as possible.

If I don't see any new sign within a step or two, I move ahead a step at a time, looking thoroughly over a half circle before moving again. I leave the spool of line at last blood and retrieve it when I find something new. If I have to backtrack far to get the string, I leave a marker at the new sign until I return. If I'm in thick cover and there is a choice of two or three trails a wounded deer may have taken, I may walk each trail for 50 yards. If I come up with nothing on any of them, I then go back and check them further. If I still come up empty, I consider a route I may have overlooked—maybe the deer backtracked.

Wounded deer sometimes circle back after going out of sight. This tactic can confuse inexperienced trackers. Also remember that seriously wounded deer tend to crash across country, even in heavy cover, rather than follow established deer trails.

A good tracker succeeds on a poor blood trail by systematically eliminating alternatives until he comes up with the right one. This often takes patience, persistence, and time. Wounded deer don't simply vanish, but they sometimes do unexpected things. Some hunters assume a deer wouldn't do this or that, so they fail to check out those possibilities, and they end up baffled. Never assume anything when tracking a wounded deer.

The animal may climb the steepest hill or mountain in the area— even though you've read they aren't supposed to do that. They may also swim or attempt to swim across a lake, pond, or river. Some wounded deer die in the water or stop on an island. Others may walk in a stream for 100 yards or more before leaving it, and may exit from the same side they entered. The only way to find where a deer leaves the water is to walk both banks both ways.

It's not unusual for injured deer to cross open fields, go into farmyards or pastures with domestic animals, or bed near houses in broad daylight. When a deer crosses a field and there's little blood, you can sometimes save time by going directly across yourself and looking for sign where the animal left the field. If there's any cover whatsoever in a field, a deer may bed down there. It doesn't take much in the way of vegetation or rocks to hide a deer that's lying down.

Leaves and pine needles sometimes have rust spots or red pigment that can be confused with blood. If in doubt, wet a finger and try to wipe the spot off. If the spot comes off, it's blood.

One fall I had the opportunity to track a wounded deer through an area that had a lot of wild grapes. Many fallen leaves were smeared by animals feeding on the grapes, and the dark juice resembled liver blood from the deer. I found it sometimes necessary to taste questionable spots because both the blood and the grape could be rubbed off. Other fruits and berries may stain leaves in much the same way.

When flecks of blood are small and hard to see, it's often wise to get on hands and knees and proceed that way. If your eyesight is poor, try to get someone with sharp eyes to accompany you. Youngsters are often good at spotting blood, and women are generally more observant than men. Penny Hickman, for example, is an important part of the team when her husband Don goes out on a blood trail because she is better at spotting blood than he is.

As you follow a blood trail, try to notice which side of the deer blood is coming from. Let's say the deer was hit on the right side, but blood always appears on the left side of the deer's route. That means there's an exit wound and it's bleeding, but the hole of entry isn't. If both entry and exit wounds are bleeding, blood will be found on both sides of the deer's trail. How high entry and exit wounds are on a deer's body can sometimes be determined by looking at the height of blood smears on trees and brush. This can be misleading, though, for blood can be thrown to the side as the animal runs.

If you find a bed vacated by a wounded deer, check where blood is located in the bed to determine or confirm where the deer might have been hit. Deer beds are roughly egg-shaped, with the wider end where the hindquarters were and the more pointed end where the front legs and chest were. If the bed is in snow, it may be possible to see the

Leaves and pine needles sometimes have rust spots that can be confused with blood. To be sure, wet a finger and try to rub off the spots.

outline of a deer's legs. Blood that is to the side, near the narrow end or front of the bed, probably originated from the deer's head or neck.

If you come to a pool of blood after finding only a steady series of drops, that's an indication the deer stopped and stood in that spot for a while before moving on. Blood accumulated there from steady dripping. A number of pools a short distance apart may indicate the deer is weakening or listening to your progress behind it before moving on. Deer that are unsteady or staggering frequently scuff up the ground and bump into trees, thus leaving blood or clumps of hair on them.

If the blood trail ends or you aren't able to find any blood to begin with, look for other sign, such as tracks or scuff marks, to determine where your deer went. A wounded deer may run for 100 yards or more before starting to bleed externally.

Here's what a bedded deer looks like. Note positioning of the body, and try to remember it the next time you examine blood sign in a vacated bed.

Dale Hulce hit a running buck one time and wasn't able to find any blood. He waited 3½ hours for the other members of his hunting party to return to camp. They then helped him look for the buck. They followed tracks and scuffed leaves for about 100 yards before finding blood. From there on, the blood trail was steady and easy to follow. The three-pointer was dead when they found it after a half-hour tracking job, a total of four hours after the buck was shot. The delay in trailing was appropriate in this case. The animal hadn't been dead long—the carcass was still limp. Dale's bullet was a gut shot, but it nicked the liver.

Hunters can get a rough idea of how long a deer has been dead by checking the degree of rigor mortis, or stiffening of the legs and jaw. According to the findings of John Gill with the Maine Department of Inland Fisheries and Wildlife and David O'Meara with the Department of Animal Pathology, in a deer that has been dead for three hours, the knees or hind-leg joints are usually stiff and can't be flexed. Front-leg joints or elbows are stiff after four hours. Rigor mortis is complete on the lower jaw two hours after death. Temperatures below freezing may quicken the stiffening of jaws and joints, making a field determination of time of death less reliable.

Running deer frequently make a noticeable disturbance on the ground every time they touch down, kicking up soil, leaves, and other debris. Kicked-up dirt may be a different color than the rest due to moisture content. By looking along the ground from a low angle, a hunter can sometimes see scuff marks or tracks that may not be visible from directly above. There are often distinct scuff marks where a deer surged away after being hit. Hair should be present on the ground at that point even if there is no blood.

It is much easier to follow the tracks of a wounded deer in sand, mud, soft ground, and snow than on rocks or hard ground. When following tracks alone, be sure to note anything peculiar about the prints that will enable you to differentiate them from others. Measure the prints if possible. Animals with back, shoulder, or leg wounds will often be using only three legs, and they may drag the fourth one. Injured deer also have a tendency to spread their hooves for added support when walking; this is something to watch for.

On hard ground, deer will sometimes disturb pebbles and small rocks, and it's possible to use this sign to follow them. Rich LaRocco hunted with one fellow who followed a wounded mule deer by feeling for slight depressions in the ground. Those tracks were actually easier to feel than to see.

Rich recommends that hunters unable to find any sign at all start a systematic search by dividing the most likely area into blocks. Corners should be selected and marked by using a compass, and the blocks should be small enough so that they can be thoroughly searched. A handmade map can be used to draw the location of each block. Then check each block off as it is searched.

Rich used this method to find a whitetail doe he arrowed in New Jersey while hunting with Jeff Anderson. As it turned out, they found the deer while marking corners of blocks to search, which Rich said happens often. If the deer isn't located in the first 10 or 20 blocks, map out another set. In time, you're bound to find the deer or some sign that will lead you to it. This method is certainly better than a haphazard, hit-or-miss type of search.

Scavenging birds, such as ravens, crows, magpies, and jays, can lead hunters to deer. These birds have excellent eyesight and are quick to spot dead and dying deer, and they can be seen in trees or brush nearby or can be heard calling to one another.

Ravens helped bowhunter Gene Stenberg find a doe he hit. Gene admits he started following the deer too soon. He and two partners jumped the whitetail and then tracked her for several hours before losing the trail. Hot and tired, they took a break and returned to the area about an hour later. When they arrived, four ravens were sitting in a tree near where the doe's trail had been lost. The hunters went to where the ravens were roosted, and after a short search found the whitetail. Another arrow was required to finish her.

The procedure John Driver used to track and recover a buck he'd hit with a rifle suggests how other hunters might proceed, and will serve as a fitting summary of and conclusion to this chapter. John saw three does first, and then he saw the buck 10 yards farther away. The antlered deer was moving through tag alders and cedars instead of along the open trail the does had taken.

John realized it would be difficult to get a bullet through the brush, but ahead he saw an opening in the cedars through which the buck would pass. He raised his scoped rifle and kept it just ahead of

Ravens, crows, and other scavenging birds quickly spot dead and dying deer and can lead hunters to animals they've hit but were unable to track due to lack of blood trail.

the whitetail. When the opening came into view, he stopped his swing. The buck's neck flashed into the scope, and John fired.

At the shot, the deer broke from a trot into a bounding run. But something about the animal's gait didn't look right. The whitetail seemed to come down gingerly right after each bound, and his tail was down. John is an experienced deer hunter, and to him, the buck looked as if it had been hit.

He hung a bright orange backpack high in a tree as a reference point, then went in the deer's general direction to look for signs of a hit. A search of the vicinity just beyond where the deer was last seen failed to turn up anything. John then returned to where he could see his pack, near where the buck was when he'd shot.

A check of that area turned up blood. The buck had been hit. John waited a half hour, then started after the deer.

Instead of continuing on its initial course, the wounded deer made a tight circle around the hunter and headed over a ridge. The blood trail wasn't heavy, so John took his time, and placed a piece of tissue paper at each spot of blood to get a line on the buck's course. He continued in a straight line from each find of blood. If no additional blood was discovered within 30 to 50 yards, he made half circles back to the last piece of tissue, first one way and then the other, until he found more blood. Sometimes he had to get down on his hands and knees to see small flecks of red.

Finally, John noticed that the deer's trail was leading into tight cover—a good place for a wounded deer to take refuge. He stood in one spot for five minutes and scoped the heavy cover. He was looking for the buck but didn't expect to see the whole animal, just something that appeared out of place.

One group of bushes seemed too thick in the middle. John concentrated his gaze on that spot and eventually made out the buck's eye, then the white patch on its throat. The tracker shot the whitetail in the neck to finish it.

4

Lung and Heart Hits

Mule deer, whitetails, and blacktails shot solidly through the heart or lungs seldom go far before dying. However, it's not unusual for deer hit through these vital organs to run out of sight before dropping. On a recent hunt out of Callaway Gardens in Georgia, for example, I shot a nine-point buck in the chest from a tree stand with a .30-06 as he stood facing me. Visibility wasn't the best, because leaves were still on the trees (it was late October). At the shot, the buck immediately took off running to the left, but it was obvious he was hit—his chest practically plowed through the ground cover because of lack of coordination and support of the front legs. Within a second or two, the deer was out of sight, giving me no chance for a second shot. It seemed the sounds of the running deer ended abruptly, so I thought it might have gone down.

The sounds of a running deer can end suddenly for a number of reasons. If my bullet had hit where I was aiming, it should have connected on the heart or lungs or both and the deer shouldn't have gone far. A hit a few inches left or right of my aiming point, however, might only have broken a shoulder—not a quick-killing shot by any means.

Darkness was only minutes away, so I climbed down as quickly as I could and walked to where I'd last seen the deer. I saw bright red blood right away, but not a lot of it, and I started following the line of

A hit in the heart/lung area usually results in a clean kill, but not always. Location of the heart on this whitetail buck is marked by *X*, and the lungs are roughly within the circle.

splotches. Within 50 yards, I found the buck piled up in a briar patch. The dense mat of leaves and stems had cushioned the deer's fall, accounting for the sudden lapse of sound. My bullet had taken away half of that buck's heart.

Deer hit through lungs or heart commonly take off running and, in fact, may show no obvious indication of being struck. Almost always, though, hair and/or blood are present to confirm a hit. Heart hits may produce a heavy blood trail if there are entry and exit holes. If there's only an entrance hole, as on that Georgia buck, there may not be much, if any, external bleeding.

In Utah one fall, Rich LaRocco was guiding a woman who was shooting a Savage .250/3000 rifle. She took a 300-yard shot at a buck standing broadside, and the muley gave no indication of being hit. But it did make a sudden change in direction at one point, starting toward one patch of cover and then suddenly turning toward a different patch. They saw the buck go into the brush, but it didn't come out.

The muley lay dead near where it had gone out of sight, shot through the heart. The bullet had gone completely through the buck, but it didn't expand and produced no blood whatsoever. The only sign of a hit Rich could find when backtracking the deer was a little hair where it had been standing at the shot.

That heart-shot buck ran an estimated 150 yards before going down. Some go farther. A deer running at top speed can cover a lot of ground in seconds. Nonetheless, most deer hit in the ticker should be on the ground within 200 yards of where they were shot. The same is true for deer on which a bullet, slug, or arrow penetrates both lungs. The prognosis changes dramatically in situations where one or both lungs are simply nicked. If only one lung is pierced, a deer can go much farther than most hunters realize, and some may even survive.

One-lung hits are common on shots taken at steep angles, either uphill or downhill, in hilly or mountainous terrain, or from elevated stands. Keep this fact in mind when you take such shots, and try to connect on both lungs by visualizing their position in the body cavity. A hunter on the ground has a much better chance of hitting both lungs than someone in an elevated position.

As mentioned in an earlier chapter, lung blood is typically red or pink in color and may contain numerous small air bubbles. If you strongly suspect you've hit a deer in the heart or lungs when hunting with a firearm, follow immediately if possible. Be sure to reload first if you're using a single-shot rifle, shotgun, or handgun. If the animal isn't found dead within a reasonable distance, the bullet, ball, or slug may have hit just one lung or struck the empty space above the lungs and below the spine. A hit in that space will do little damage, and the animal has a good chance of recovering.

In either event, trail the deer as far as possible. If the blood trail is sparse and/or you're having doubts about where your shot hit, it may be a good idea to back off and get help before trying to follow farther. Even if you plan to continue trailing a lung-hit deer yourself, it is sometimes best to wait an hour or more for the animal to weaken. The same advice applies if you are confident of a hit in the chest cavity but have found no blood to confirm it.

Russ Greenwood, with Doonan Gulch Outfitters in Broadus, Montana, put in almost a full day to recover a 4 x 4 muley buck wounded by one of his clients. The buck was shot at 9:00 A.M. with a 100-grain bullet out of a 6 mm. rifle as it angled toward the hunter. The bullet broke a front leg and caught the bottom of one lung. It was late November with a wind-chill registering 30 degrees below zero, and there was snow on the ground.

Russ tracked the buck until noon and jumped it from three beds, but the muley was alert enough to stay ahead of him far enough that no shot was possible. The guide said there was good blood for the first hour of tracking, but then it dropped off due to the cold temperature. He took a break for lunch, then resumed tracking the injured muley.

Wind had blown the tracks away where Russ had left them, but he knew where the buck was headed and picked up the tracks again in a timbered ravine where there was protection from the wind. There were three beds in a small area where the buck had shifted positions, but it then left as the guide approached. Russ finally intercepted the buck at 3:00 P.M. by circling uphill and ahead of it. The muley had covered 3½ miles from the spot where it was originally hit.

The lung injury appeared to have had little impact on this buck because the organ was just grazed. The deer acted as if it simply had a broken leg. If there had been no snow, it would have been advisable to get help after the deer was jumped the first time, positioning hunters where they might get a shot when it was jumped again. And if there hadn't been snow, it would have been difficult to stay on its trail when the wound stopped bleeding.

Even a deer hit through both lungs may require another shot, so always be ready to shoot again. Hans Klein from New York State recovered a whitetail three hours after it had been shot through the lungs with a shotgun slug. The deer went only about 150 yards, but it was still on its feet when Hans shot it a second time.

Bowhunters who suspect they have put an arrow into the heart or lungs of a deer should wait 30 to 60 minutes before starting to trail the animal—unless they see or hear the deer go down and believe it's dead. In the event of a sudden rain shower or snow flurries and in the absence of a string tracker, you may have to start trailing sooner or risk having the blood trail washed away or covered.

There are a number of good reasons for gun hunters to actively try to recover deer they've hit, as compared to the passive approach usually recommended for bowhunters. The reasons are directly linked to the differences between guns and bows and the impacts of bullets vs. broadheads. The shock and tissue damage from a bullet may disable and/or disorient a deer quick enough and long enough for a hunter who follows immediately to get another crack at it. Also, it's easier to make followup shots at deer with firearms than with archery equipment; guns have greater range, and shots can be taken through small openings.

It's difficult under the best of circumstances to put a second arrow into a wounded deer; bowhunters who follow immediately risk pushing an animal farther than it probably would have gone if left undisturbed, perhaps increasing the difficulty of recovering it. Archery tackle is quiet compared to firearms, and arrows don't deliver the shock that bullets do. Consequently, an arrowed deer that is seriously injured will often travel only a short distance before lying down, and it will eventually bleed to death. A properly placed, sharp broadhead will kill a deer in seconds, but death comes slower on hits that are a little off, like those that take out only one lung. It's far better to wait longer than you may think you have to before following an arrowed deer than not to wait long enough.

A bowhunter who scores a hit need not spend all his waiting time in one place. Time often passes quicker if you leave your stand and return later. You may want to use the time to get help, get a camera, or eat a meal. If you do leave the area, though, do so as quietly as possible to avoid disturbing the animal, which may be bedded nearby.

If you do see the deer you hit lie down within sight, remain quietly where you are and keep an eye on it until it expires, or try to shoot it again if a shot is possible. Michigan bowhunter Dave Borgeson arrowed an eight-point buck through one lung a number of years ago and watched it walk a short distance and lie down. The buck's head stayed up and it remained alert for about 20 minutes, so Dave took a long second shot. That shaft hit low, striking a foot.

The buck got up and walked a short distance before lying down again. It was far enough away by then that Dave was able to sneak out of there. He returned at 1:00 P.M. (the whitetail had been first hit at 8:00 A.M.), located a few beds where the buck had lain, then saw it run ahead of him and jump a fence. He left the area again, returning at 4:00 P.M. to find the buck dead 50 yards beyond the fence.

Dave's original broadhead had cut the liver and spleen in addition to the one lung. He attributed the buck's endurance to the fact that it walked rather than ran after being hit, and it didn't walk far before bedding. Because it didn't exert itself, the buck was able to maintain energy for a long period. Adult bucks are often tougher to kill with marginal hits than are does and younger deer of either sex because of their greater size and stamina, and that probably was another factor in this case.

It would have been a mistake to try to push that deer rather than wait it out. The whitetail bled heavily at first, but that didn't last long. A steady trailing effort may have pushed the buck farther than it could easily have been followed. There was also the potential of pushing it onto private property where access may not have been guaranteed.

New Yorker Don Hickman used a dog to track a bow-shot eight-pointer hit through both lungs. That whitetail covered 1½ miles. The bowhunter who hit it waited three hours, trailed it 250 to 300 yards, then called Don for help.

Don and his dog tracked the buck another 300 yards when he spotted a deer 40 yards ahead that ran off looking healthy. However, after 200 more yards it let Don get within 25 feet. When jumped a third

Gene Lengsfeld shows the mounted head of a Boone and Crockett buck he got with bow and arrow in Minnesota. Gene's arrow hit only one lung, and the deer ran three fourths of a mile before dropping.

time, the deer ran into a trailer park, bounced off a mailbox, and entered private property where Don didn't have permission to follow.

The necessary permission was secured the following morning, and the buck was found dead where it had bedded once again after crossing a cut cornfield. Don commented that if he had waited until that morning to begin tracking rather than starting the evening before, he probably would have found the buck dead within 400 yards of where it was first hit instead of 1½ miles away.

Two other dog handlers from New York—Hans Klein and Roger Humeston—recovered a four-point buck on which one lung had been punctured by an arrow. The shaft penetrated eight to nine inches down through the back. That buck covered a number of miles before they caught up to it. Then they shot it again to put it down for keeps.

Former Minnesota resident Gene Lengsfeld bow-bagged a big buck with a typical Boone and Crockett rack carrying 12 points that stood as a state record for a year. His arrow caught one lung, and the buck ran about three-fourths of a mile at top speed before collapsing. Fortunately, there was snow on the ground, so Gene could track the buck the entire distance. He said there was a good blood trail for the first half mile, but it tapered off beyond that. The record-book buck followed an open lane for almost the entire distance, then staggered 20 yards off to the side before dying. This is another example of how a big buck's will to live carried it farther than normal.

To reach the lung area, bowhunters should always try to place arrows behind the shoulder blades; those heavy bones frequently stop broadheads, preventing them from doing much damage. However, some shoulder-blade hit deer are recoverable. Scott Hannuksela put a broadhead far enough through the shoulder blade of a doe to clip one lung. Luckily, there was snow that enabled him to follow the deer far enough to recover it.

The arrow from Scott's 55-pound-pull bow may have actually cracked or broken the shoulder blade, because the whitetail dragged her left front leg as she walked. It was apparent that this deer was seriously hurt; she fell or lay down twice within a short distance of where she was hit, and Scott's arrow remained in the deer. Arrows typically fall out of a shoulder-hit deer within a short distance because they seldom penetrate far. Deer that aren't seriously injured usually continue walking without lying down.

Bowhunters who suspect they've connected on a shoulder blade and believe their arrow may have gone in far enough to get one lung should wait up to four hours before starting to track the animal— provided rain or snow isn't a problem. After that time, if the animal is

The deer's heavy shoulder blade stops many broadheads, but some go through far enough to damage one lung.

jumped but a finishing shot isn't possible, leave the deer again for a number of hours; it probably won't go far before lying down again and weakening further.

After jumping his deer for the second time, Scott backed off and left it for several hours before returning with his father, Paul, and a friend, Rob. They jumped the doe again, and they could see she was weakening because she lay down again within sight. The hunters decided to try to finish her as soon as possible because of her condition and because the snow cover would enable them to stay on her tail even if the bleeding stopped. Her dragging left front leg was distinct enough to enable them to separate her tracks from those of other deer.

Both Scott and Rob were of high-school age and in good shape. The plan was for them to sneak up on the bedded deer and try to shoot it again. If the doe moved out before that was possible, they would push as fast as possible until they got close enough for another shot.

The deer moved out ahead of them, and they tore after it—making sure all arrows were safely in their quivers. The doe stayed ahead for about a mile, then became too weak to continue. That tracking effort covered at least two miles from start to finish.

If a bullet or arrow goes through the chest cavity but passes through the void above the lungs, missing them entirely, it can be difficult to recover the deer. If there's no lung blood, bleeding gradually tapers off, and the deer acts healthy, that chest space may be where your shot hit. Deer can recover from an injury of this type, but still you must follow as far as possible. The next chapter covers the recovery of a deer shot in that area.

5

Trail of a Wounded Whitetail

As sometimes happens in bowhunting, Bruce Dupras's arrow hit a branch when he took a shot at a whitetail. A deflected arrow often results in a miss, and that's what Bruce thought he got. But it wasn't. We eventually located bright red drops of blood on the snow in the direction the deer ran after the shot.

Dupras is my brother-in-law. He and his 12-year-old son Jason were hunting with me during late December in Michigan when Bruce's deflected arrow struck the deer. It was Jason's first year of deer hunting, and the whitetail his father hit set the stage for the boy to learn some valuable lessons that should stay with him for life.

About an hour after the hit, the three of us started following the blood trail. The drops were steady, and the deer's course was easy to trace. After covering about 200 yards, the animal lay down in thick spruces, but got up without our seeing it. From the position of the blood in the bed, it was obvious the deer had been hit high.

It was also apparent that the arrow had probably missed heart and lungs. If the whitetail had been hit in those vital organs, it would not have been alert enough to move off ahead of us undetected. However, the fact that it had bedded quickly indicated it might be seriously hurt.

If there had been no snow, we probably would have left the trail

There's a void above the lungs and below the backbone of deer. A hit here may not be fatal, but deer hit there can occasionally be recovered. The X marks the spot hunters should try to avoid.

and returned the next morning, reducing the chances of pushing the animal farther than we might be able to follow it. Given the snow cover, we could continue and better assess the situation without concern about losing the trail.

We jumped the deer from two more beds in the next half mile. I caught a glimpse of it ahead of us at one point, but I didn't see it well enough to determine the extent of its injury. But its tracks told a story of their own. The whitetail started a series of bounds, always slowing to a walk after running a short distance. It was hurting.

As darkness neared, the whitetail crossed a frozen river, and we decided to leave its trail there. The spot would be easy to find in the morning. The sky was clear and no snow was forecast, so there was no worry about the deer's trail being covered.

It was a good thing we stopped where we did because it took us at least an hour to return to the road where our vehicle was parked. We covered most of the distance in the dark, and a compass came in handy. It's easy to lose track of direction when following a wounded deer, especially where we were hunting in the rugged Upper Peninsula. Although the area was laced with logging roads, there were miles of swamp between them in some places.

Bruce had to work the next day, so Jason and I returned to continue after the deer. I was confident the animal had bedded down soon after we had left its trail the evening before, and I wouldn't have been surprised to find it dead.

I was right about the deer bedding down. Soon after resuming the wounded whitetail's trail, I noticed the animal wasn't bleeding as much as it had been initially. Drops of blood stained the snow less frequently, but there was still enough to enable us to easily follow the animal—red shows up well on white.

The deer's next bedding place was a surprise, and we were caught off guard. I was also surprised that the deer was very much alive.

The blood trail led through a narrow band of thick cover bordering the river and into an opening with a small patch of cover in the center. The deer's tracks led toward the clump of cover, which I thought was a perfect place for an injured animal to lie in and be able to watch its backtrail. But the deer wasn't there. I assumed it had continued across the opening to the woods on the other side. That assumption made me careless, and I didn't notice its tracks turn toward a brushpile in the opening. When we blundered past it, the deer jumped up and bounded across the opening to where I assumed it had already gone.

If I had been ready with an arrow on the string, as I should have been, I could at least have gotten a shot. The snow was deep enough to slow the deer's progress. And if I had been paying attention a bit earlier, I may have gotten a poke at the deer while it was still bedded.

My carelessness cost us a chance to end the tracking job quickly.

Bruce's arrow was still in the deer; I noted its location as the animal ran off. Placement appeared to be behind the shoulder blade but a little high. The shaft certainly had missed the lungs and all major blood vessels, probably entering the empty space void of vitals above a deer's lungs and below the backbone.

But I wasn't ready to give up yet. As long as the shaft was in the deer, there was a chance it might do more damage, especially while the animal was running hard. The whitetail was a small one, too, meaning it would weaken faster than an adult would. The energy it expended running from us was bound to take its toll.

I'm a stickler when it comes to wounded deer. Once a deer is injured, by myself or someone in my party, I'm not willing to give up until all prospects of recovering the animal have been exhausted. I consider an arrow in the chest cavity a serious injury even if the lungs are missed, especially with the shaft remaining in place.

The deer's exertion brought on renewed bleeding, another positive sign. This was Jason's first real trailing experience, and I tried to explain to him my interpretations of what was happening as we followed the wounded whitetail. Above all else, I wanted to instill optimism in our prospects of success, to keep his interest up. Far too many hunters give up too soon on wounded deer, and I didn't want him to fit in that category.

Why do hunters quit earlier than they should? Many become convinced they won't succeed, or they lack the ability to follow an injured deer far. Others fear becoming lost if they venture far from their stand or a road, or are out of shape and simply incapable of following a deer far. Worst of all, I suspect that some hunters don't think enough of their quarry to put in a serious effort to recover it—especially if it is a small or antlerless deer.

Any person with such an attitude is not a hunter. There is no excuse for taking a shot, with gun or bow, at a deer if you are not willing to exert every effort possible to recover it. No one likes to wound a deer, but it does happen occasionally, often because of factors beyond a hunter's control, as in Bruce's case. Incidentally, Bruce said he would have taken a day off work to trail that deer if I hadn't been available to help. All deer hunters should have that attitude. Or, at the very least, they should be extra careful about taking shots on their last evening of hunting, taking only those that are most likely to result in clean kills.

When Jason and I jumped it, Bruce's deer stopped running soon after it went out of sight. The arrow probably made running uncomfortable. By then it was apparent to me that pushing the deer in an effort to weaken it was the best strategy, and that's what we did. We jumped the whitetail from beds on a regular basis, but it always managed to slip out ahead of us in the thick cover.

The arrow finally fell out of the deer about a mile from where we'd jumped it that morning. Bleeding slowed thereafter, but I caught a glimpse of the animal soon after we found the shaft. Jason was beginning to have doubts about recovery of the deer, primarily because he was tiring from the exertion of trudging through snow that was more than a foot deep. But I urged him on, confident we were getting close to the end of the trail.

The deer was lying down more often.

Not long afterward, I spotted the whitetail bedded ahead of us. The animal was rapidly running out of steam. I pointed it out to Jason, then tried to maneuver into position for a shot. The deer got up before that was possible, but I could still see it when it lay down again. I finally got the chance I wanted, and finished the button buck with another arrow.

Some 2½ hours had elapsed since we'd left the vehicle at 9:30 A.M. The effort had been work, but it was worth it and I believe Jason felt the same. There is satisfaction in following a blood trail to the end. The harder the trail, the more satisfaction.

As I dressed the young buck, my suspicions about the placement of Bruce's deflected arrow were confirmed. His broadhead had missed all organs and major blood vessels. It had done enough damage, though, to weaken the animal enough to enable us eventually to catch up to it. I was thankful for the snow.

However, the task was far from complete. We had to get the deer back to the vehicle. We hadn't crossed a road or trail all morning and would have to use a compass to find our way back. I had taken a compass reading when we'd left the car and river and had checked it periodically during the morning. The deer had led us just about straight north.

The river was south, but my vehicle was parked to the west, so we angled off in a southwesterly direction, hoping to hit the road before we reached the river. Another option would have been to backtrack ourselves in the snow.

The snow made dragging the deer easier, but the thick swamps we had to navigate offset some of that advantage. I was glad the whitetail wasn't larger. In time we came to an old logging road. I knew it probably led to a plowed road, but I wasn't sure which direction to take. Some logging roads meander about like a feeding deer. Not wanting to drag the deer in the wrong direction, we left it on the edge of the logging road and headed west on the trail, planning to return for it after locating a drivable road.

Our choice of direction proved wrong. The trail petered out in a swamp after about a mile. We had made some southerly progress, so we continued south and eventually reached the river. It was 4:30 by the time we got back to the vehicle. We were both tired, hungry, and thirsty—we'd neglected to carry snack foods along, as we should have. Since it would soon be dark, we decided to retrieve the deer the next day. The dressed carcass would be fine, with temperatures well below freezing.

We brought snowshoes with us the next day to make walking

Jason Dupras drags a recovered deer out on a sled with the help of snowshoes.

easier, plus a sled on which to drag the deer. As it turned out, the logging road where we had left the deer didn't connect with the main road, so we simply headed east until hitting it. Our tracks from the previous day identified the right trail. We had left the deer only about ¾-of-a-mile east of the main road. With a packed snowshoe trail to follow and the help of the sled, the deer was easy to drag to the road.

Although Jason wasn't too crazy about the work involved, he now looks back on the experience with a smile. He learned a number of important lessons during those days. At the top of the list is the fact that poorly hit deer can go a long way, so it's important to take only good shots that are likely to hit vital areas and result in clean kills. Other lessons are that deer are sometimes wounded, that every effort should be made to recover a hit animal, and that it is possible if you are persistent.

He also saw firsthand how to navigate across country through roadless land without getting lost. However, I'm sure he had doubts a time or two about my ability to use a compass!

The evening of that same day a stroke of luck enabled Jason to bag his first whitetail under unique circumstances. We hung Bruce's deer from a tree and spent the rest of the day hunting in an area that had been recently logged. At dusk we encountered a young doe that had crawled under a slash pile to feed on browse and got stuck there. It surely would have died a slow death if Jason hadn't stumbled across it.

6

Head and Neck Hits

Properly placed head and neck shots should be instantly fatal with firearms and nearly so with bow and arrow. The problem with aiming at these parts of a deer's anatomy is there is little margin for error. The kill zone is small, requiring accurate shooting. If an animal moves its head or neck at the wrong instant or if the shot is off target, hunters can be in for a long tracking job.

In my opinion, bowhunters should never take a head shot; it's also a poor choice for gun hunters. Bullets or slugs that miss their mark on a head shot often break the lower jaw. A deer injured in this fashion, unless the hunter can successfully track it down, is doomed to a slow death because it will be unable to eat.

Guide Dan Massee, with C Lazy Three Outfitters based in Ovando, Montana, helped one of his clients recover a mule deer on which the lower jaw had been shot off. There was no snow, and they blood-trailed the muley as far as possible, jumping it from at least one bed. The buck had been working its way uphill, so when Dan lost its trail, he circled uphill ahead of it to a vantage point from which he was able to spot the injured buck with binoculars. His client then shot the buck again.

Don Hickman, President of Deer Search, Inc., in New York, tracked a jaw-hit whitetail buck with one of his dogs for 17 hours. He

The head-neck area is not the best choice of targets. There isn't much margin for error. However, if hit properly there, deer die instantly.

started after the buck one evening and followed it until after dark, then resumed tracking the next day at 7:00 A.M. The deer was jumped within 300 yards of where the track had been left the night before, and a hunter got a shot at it shortly afterward but missed.

Another hunter eventually put the buck down for keeps about 4:00 P.M. Don said the blood sign from the jaw wound was very distinctive, appearing in long strings. The blood was actually mixed with saliva.

Whenever you take a head or neck shot, keep the deer covered and be ready for a second shot even if it collapses instantly. The shock of a bullet or slug striking a nonfatal blow to those areas can temporarily

Binoculars can help you spot wounded deer whose trail has been lost.

stun a deer, knocking it off its feet for up to 10 minutes. I know of several cases in which bucks were hit in the antlers and knocked unconscious, only to recover and escape by catching hunters off-guard. The same thing can happen if the skull is grazed or there's a near miss on the neck bone.

Michigan deer hunter Chum Steinhoff, for example, shot a six-point buck with a muzzle-loading rifle one time at a distance of 200 feet, and it dropped in its tracks. Confident that he'd killed the deer, Steinhoff didn't bother to reload, leaving the blackpowder rifle in his blind and walking to the deer. When he reached the buck, he tagged it, noticing there was some eye and tail movement.

After the tag was in place, Steinhoff grabbed the buck by an antler and started to pull if off to the side to dress it. At that point, the hunter got one of the biggest surprises of his hunting career. The buck suddenly came to, jumped to its feet, and started walking off wearing Steinhoff's tag.

Fortunately, the deer didn't go far before falling again, and Steinhoff finished it with his knife. He would have been much better prepared, however, had he reloaded his rifle and carried it with him to the downed buck. The movements the animal made when he reached it should have been a giveaway that it wasn't dead yet. The lead ball from Steinhoff's rifle had hit the buck at the base of the antlers, stunning it.

This hunter was lucky the deer didn't get away, and even luckier that he wasn't injured. Finishing a still-struggling deer with a knife is not a recommended practice. The hooves and antlers of deer can inflict severe injuries, and these animals can be extremely strong, regardless of their size.

A hunter can avoid unnecessary surprises like that one by always keeping his gun loaded and ready for use until he knows beyond doubt that a deer is dead. Get up next to a fallen deer as quickly as possible, provided you can keep the animal in sight as you approach. If you will lose sight of the animal during your approach, it's best to stay where you can watch it and shoot again, if necessary, until you're sure it's dead.

The first thing I do upon reaching a fallen deer is visually confirm the location of my shot. Blood is usually visible at the location of a hit. I also look for eye movement and signs of breathing. The eyes of a dead deer will be wide open and motionless. Breathing can be detected by looking at a deer's side. I always shoot again if there's any chance a deer might get up, based on hit location and its actions.

It's not unusual for dying deer to make some movement when they are down. By determining where the animal was hit, it's normally possible to differentiate between muscle contractions and the deer's potential ability to get back up and try to escape. Nonetheless, always remain ready to shoot until all movement ceases and a deer is definitely dead.

Bowhunters who drop a deer instantly with a neck hit should put an insurance arrow into the animal, aiming for the lungs. It's extremely difficult to connect with a second arrow after a stunned deer recovers, regains its feet, and starts moving away. Wait at least an hour before trailing a neck-shot deer that runs out of sight and hearing. If the jugular vein is cut, a deer should be dead in less than 200 yards, but it won't die as quickly from a sliced windpipe.

A New York hunter arrowed a deer in the neck, cutting the windpipe, and he started following it immediately. The deer was jumped within a short distance and made a mad dash away from its pursuer. There was a poor blood trail because the broadhead had missed the carotid arteries.

It was the following day before the buck was located, 500 yards from where it had been hit. The deer had gone into a lake because it had been pressured and was just offshore. The carcass was bloated and the meat beyond salvage. If the hunter had been more patient, he may have found the animal dead in its first bed.

Coyotes sometimes beat hunters to wounded deer.

Gun hunters who hit a deer in the windpipe and aren't able to recover it with an immediate followup, then run out of daylight, should probably wait until the next day to recover the animal, weather permitting. Bright red and/or pink blood containing big air bubbles may result from a severed windpipe. It may also be possible to hear the animal's labored breathing.

One hunter who hit a six-point buck in the windpipe with a shotgun slug said it sounded as if the deer was growling. The buck was hit late in the day, so the hunter got a flashlight and started trailing it. He jumped the buck and then lost its trail. A tracking dog was called in, and the buck was encountered standing half a mile from where the hunter had lost the trail. Another shot put the buck down. If the hunter had waited until the next morning to track the deer, it may have been dead, and if it wasn't, he would have had a good chance of finishing it himself.

Coyotes beat Wyoming guide and outfitter Maury Jones to a mule deer buck that one of his clients had neck-shot with an arrow. They waited 50 minutes after the deer was hit before starting to track it. Jones said there was a lot of blood for the first 100 yards, but then the sign dropped off dramatically, with a drop only every 25 yards or so. They trailed the buck for three hours, covering about three-quarters of a mile, before quitting for the day.

The next morning they heard coyotes howling in the direction the buck had gone. They found what was left of the carcass in the next canyon. It wasn't clear whether the coyotes had found the buck dead or had killed it themselves. The muley's neck had been fed upon, so it was impossible to determine what damage the arrow had done.

Maury estimated the buck had traveled about a mile from where it was hit and had stayed on its feet the entire distance. The buck also had stayed on the same level of a mountain slope, not going up or downhill.

Losing part or all of a deer to scavengers such as coyotes and bears is always a possibility wherever they coexist with deer and a lot of time elapses between a hit and recovery. I know of cases in which badgers have claimed hunter-hit deer, burying most of the carcass. This is another reason to try to recover injured deer as soon as possible. However, the presence of scavengers shouldn't be used as an excuse to follow an injured deer too soon. The loss of deer to coyotes, badgers, or bears happens in only a small percentage of cases.

7

Back Hits

Most back hits are probably high hits from bullets or broadheads intended for the shoulder area. There's no problem if the backbone is broken, but there can be if a shot misses just above the spine. In either event, deer generally go down on the spot. Those whose spines are broken are down for keeps. Near misses temporarily stun deer from a few seconds to as long as 10 minutes, and they will get up and run off if not shot again. Although spine-shot deer are not capable of getting up, their heads usually remain up and they often pull themselves along with their front legs.

Deer with broken backs should be shot a second time, either in the neck or behind the shoulder in the heart/lung area. Take a neck shot only with a gun and if you're close enough and accurate enough to insure a solid hit in the center of the neck. The deer's neck must be stationary. One time, when hunting with a rifle, I tried to neck-shoot a buck with a broken back as it struggled to get up, its head and neck bobbing from side to side. The shot missed. The next round went in behind the shoulder. That's the spot bowhunters should aim for when following up on a spine-shot deer.

Because it is usually impossible to determine whether the spine is broken or the deer is just stunned, and because deer hit high in the back can be difficult to recover, all deer dropped with a back injury should be given a second shot as quickly as possible. A quick follow-

A hit anywhere along the spine *(marked by X's)* **stuns a deer, but if the spine isn't broken, the animal will get up and run off.**

up shot puts potentially wounded deer in the same category with those that have broken backs—dead.

Unfortunately, some hunters every year fail to follow that advice. Some of them honestly feel a deer is down for keeps, drop their guard, and so are unprepared when a deer recovers from being stunned. Others don't want to "waste" another shell or arrow or "ruin any meat." Still others have an ego problem and are more concerned about claiming a "one-shot kill" than a quick, clean kill. With many back hits, two shots produce a quicker, cleaner kill than one.

Those hunters who hold their fire because of concern about using ammo unnecessarily may end up expending more than two rounds to eventually recover a wounded deer. Ammunition and arrows are necessary for hunters to secure deer. Those who are hesitant to use them should do their shooting on a target range rather than in the deer

It's important to keep your sights on deer that drop right away and to shoot again if they move.

woods. Hunters should always carry spare ammunition and arrows to finish a wounded deer, especially in areas where the terrain is open and long shots are common.

Hunters who are worried about a followup shot ruining meat should get a supply from a supermarket rather than hunt for it. Failure to take a second shot on a deer hit in the back may result in loss of a deer and no meat whatsoever. The fact is, little meat is ruined when a deer is shot in the neck or behind the shoulder.

Any such reasoning that increases the chances of a deer running off wounded qualifies as false conservation. There is no room for that type of thinking among deer hunters.

It should be pointed out that deer hit anywhere along the back close to the spine will react in basically the same way. They will drop immediately, though they may get up after the shock of a near miss of the spine. Blood sign is often sparse and of muscle origin. Blood smeared on brush and trees should be three to four feet above ground level, depending upon the size of the deer.

The following examples should help illustrate the necessity of quick followup shots on back-hit deer. A number of years ago my brother shot a beautiful eight-point buck with a musket. The buck went down, got up a couple of times, but fell back down. Bruce didn't reload, confident it would soon be dead. However, when the buck regained its feet the third time, it walked off. Bruce reloaded as rapidly as possible.

I wasn't far from Bruce when he shot, so I went to check on his success. He had just finished reloading when I reached him, and we started following the buck right away. Fortunately, there was snow, for the blood tapered off to nothing and all we had to follow were the buck's tracks. A lot of deer tracks were in the area, but the buck's prints were distinctive because he was dragging his feet more than a healthy deer would, and he was favoring a front leg.

I saw the buck after a short distance, but Bruce wasn't in position for a shot. The whitetail was on his feet and looked healthy as he ran off. I followed the buck's tracks as Bruce paralleled me off to the side, looking for the deer ahead and to the sides of us. A deer that knows it's being followed will often hook to the left or right before stopping or lying down to watch its backtrack.

We had covered at least half a mile and were in a thick swamp when Bruce said, "What's that up ahead? Is that him?"

I saw a deer standing broadside, but I had to crouch low to see its head and confirm the presence of antlers. "That's him! Take him!" Seconds later, the trophy buck was his.

Over the years, we've learned to be careful when tracking wounded deer to be sure we shoot the right one. Wounded animals often seek out healthy ones, and it's not unusual to see them before you spot the one you're after. If you're not careful, you may shoot the wrong deer.

Bruce Smith follows bloodless tracks of an eight-point buck he hit high in the back with a musket ball.

If snow hadn't been present, there's a good chance we wouldn't have recovered that buck. But I doubt the back wound alone would have killed that deer. Of course, if Bruce had reloaded right away and shot the buck a second time, tracking it would have been unnecessary. He has never repeated that mistake.

Although high back hits may not prove fatal, they can slow the animals down enough to give hunters another crack. And it is to a hunter's advantage to make the second chance count because there may not be a third. New York's John Jeanneney is one of the original members of Deer Search, Inc., a group of volunteers who use trained

Bruce Smith with the buck we recovered by teaming up to follow it in the snow.

dogs to track wounded deer. John got a call from a conservation officer one time for assistance in locating a whitetail that had been illegally shot with a shotgun during bow season. The deer had been hit high in the back.

The officer saw the hunter shoot the deer, but he thought the buck was hit better than it was. The CO needed the deer as evidence.

John's dog had tracked the injured buck for about two miles when they came upon it bedded 30 feet away. The officer had only his .38 caliber service revolver; he was still convinced they would find the buck dead. A .38 is inadequate as a deer gun, but the CO took several shots and hit the deer each time. Those shots seemed to have little effect. John and the officer followed the buck another two miles before giving up.

The blood trail was poor, too, and without the dog, they wouldn't have been able to track the deer nearly as far as they did.

Almost 1½ boxes of rifle shells went into the final recovery of another eight-point buck hit high in the back. The buck was shot late one evening and dropped instantly. But it got back up and was gone before the hunter could reach it. Snow enabled the hunter and his brother to track the buck the next morning despite a poor to nonexistent blood trail. This buck was dragging a front leg, probably due to nerve damage, enabling them to stay on the right track.

The buck bedded a number of times; seeing it now and then, the trailing hunters took seven shots, all misses. An undetermined number of miles were covered during the tracking effort. I learned about the wounded buck that evening and resumed tracking the buck the next morning along with another member of the party.

The buck was in a remote area with few roads, so we made arrangements to signal our location with three shots, when and if we got the deer, so other members of the party could help drag the whitetail to a road. Other hunters were positioned where they might intercept the buck if we didn't get it. After tracking the buck about a mile, we jumped it at close range. My partner fired three times, and I shot once.

One of the shots connected, killing the buck. The tally of shots taken to anchor the deer came to 12. Then we started firing signal shots and expended an additional 16 rounds. In this case, a quick second shot could have saved 26 others. The signal shots weren't really necessary. My partner and I could and should have dragged the deer out ourselves, and that's what I will do under similar circumstances in the future.

Plenty of hunting experience enabled 71-year-old Floyd Ferguson to recover a big buck he hit high in the back, just in front of the hindquarters. He shot the buck about 8:00 A.M. and followed it until 10:30, finally losing the trail. The buck wasn't leaving much of a blood trail, but Floyd tracked it about 1½ miles.

The deer was headed north when he lost it, so he decided to circle ahead, hoping to see the buck or some sign of its passing. He walked

Lennie Rezmer approaches an eight-point buck on which his arrow cut the aortic artery below the backbone. The buck bedded next to the clump of small-leafed trees directly behind Lennie and died after walking a short distance from that bed.

for five minutes to the west, then five minutes north, and was in the process of going the same distance to the east when he spotted the whitetail 50 to 60 yards away. A 165-grain bullet from his .264 magnum rifle anchored the buck with a heart shot.

On rare occasions, deer hit high in the back aggravate the injury as they run off. That's what happened in a situation involving New Yorker Don Hickman. A friend of Don's son hit a spike buck high in the back with an arrow. The blood trail petered out after about 200 yards.

One of Don's dogs was brought in, and the buck was located 200 yards beyond the end of the blood trail where it had jumped a fence. The shock of landing after the leap cracked the arrow-weakened spine, and the buck was unable to get back up.

Shots that hit deer directly under the spine usually kill quickly because the aortic artery is located there, paralleling the backbone from the shoulder back to the hindquarters. There's usually a good—and short—trail of bright red blood. This large blood vessel and the spine are so close together that a bullet or slug that cuts it often breaks the back, too. That isn't as likely with a broadhead.

Take the eight-pointer Lennie Rezmer arrowed during a recent November, for example. The hit was actually a potential gut shot, but because his Terminator broadhead severed the aortic artery, a clean kill resulted. The arrow entered the buck's right side and didn't exit. Typical of arterial wounds, blood sprayed far to the side of the buck's tracks as it ran.

The whitetail ran about 200 yards and bedded. For some unknown reason, it then stood up and started walking, but it covered barely 10 yards before falling dead. Uncertain about the type of hit he had, Lennie waited about three hours before starting to follow the deer. The animal probably died within minutes of being hit, but Lennie did the right thing based on where he saw his arrow hit. As stated earlier, it's far better to wait longer than necessary than not long enough.

8

Liver and Kidney Hits

One of my first experiences with a liver hit involved a nice mule deer with 5 x 6 antlers that I shot in Colorado while hunting with guide and outfitter Rudy Rudibaugh. I fired as the buck was moving at a fast walk above timberline at a range of 200 to 250 yards, but I didn't lead him enough to get the lungs. My 150-grain .30-06 slug hit the deer in the center of the body, damaging the liver.

I was more excitable and less experienced then. The terrain was open enough that I could watch the buck's progress after the hit, and I saw him go down in a thick patch of willows. Anxious to claim my first big muley, I raced to the spot. The buck reacted to my sudden appearance by jumping up and bouncing downhill, and I began trying to hit the moving target at close range with my variable scope still set on nine power. In my excitement, I forgot to turn the scope's magnification down to three power.

I had a hard enough time finding the deer in the scope, much less hitting it. The buck was hurt bad enough that it didn't go far before dropping into the willows again. I pressed my pursuit, jumping the buck once more and missing with another volley of shots. The buck went down for a third time, and I was able to finish it.

By then I was about done in, too, from chasing the buck at about 10,000 feet of elevation. I also had 12 fewer shells than I had started

The two *X*'s on this mule deer show approximate locations of the liver and kidney. The liver is in the middle of the body and the kidney high in front of the hindquarter.

with, and the buck had one less antler point, knocked off by one of my errant shots. I had the buck, but a different approach would have accomplished the same thing and been easier on me and my ammunition supply. I could have remained where I'd shot for an hour, keeping an eye on where the buck went down and then moving in. If the buck wasn't yet dead, I probably could have finished him quickly.

An alternative almost as good would have been to move in slowly on the bedded buck, increasing the chances of catching it by surprise. That approach would have given me time to calm down and think, so I probably would have readjusted my scope magnification and increased the odds of my hitting the buck if he ran.

The open terrain gave me an edge that I didn't fully take advantage of then but will in the future under similar circumstances. If you can watch an injured buck bed down, you can keep an eye on it until it dies or carefully plan a stalk.

Getting back to liver wounds—they normally prove fatal. It can take a while for a liver-hit deer to die, however, like my first big muley. A major blood vessel enters the liver, and if it's severed, death often comes quickly. If only one of its lobes is damaged, as is most commonly the case, it takes longer for an animal to succumb.

Dark red blood originates from the liver, but damage to muscles and blood vessels may also cause bright red blood at the same time.

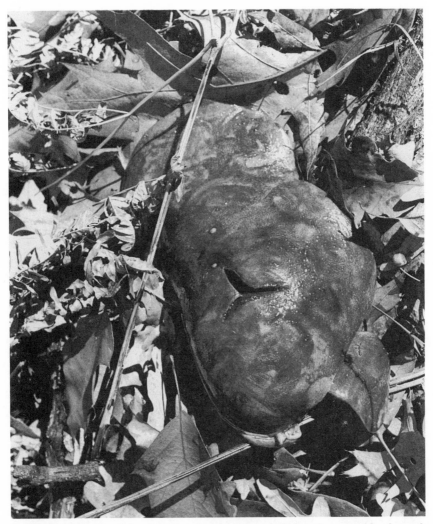

A cut made through a lobe of the liver by a broadhead. Unless the major blood vessel supplying the liver is severed, it can take an hour or two for liver-hit deer to die.

Gun hunters can try their best to quickly finish a liver-hit deer, but if they fail, it is advisable to wait an hour or two before following farther. Bowhunters should wait about two hours before starting after a liver-hit deer, weather permitting.

The year after I shot my first muley, I hunted the same area with Rudy again. California bowhunter Bill German was on that same hunt, and he liver-shot a buck with 3 x 3 antlers after stalking to within 30 yards of it. Not sure exactly where his arrow had hit, and finding a good blood trail, Bill and his father and Rudy started trailing the buck right away. The deer dropped down from the willows into timber, so the men were unable to keep it in sight.

The blood trail got skimpy after they jumped the muley from a bed, and the hunters were almost ready to give up hope when they

Bill German poses with the 3 x 3 mule deer he got in Colorado with a liver shot. His father is kneeling behind him.

found the deer dead on the downhill side of the timber. About two hours had elapsed, and the buck had covered about half a mile. That deer would have died in its first bed if the hunters had waited before trailing it.

Wounded deer that go downhill sometimes build up momentum that carries them farther than they would normally go, especially on steep slopes. Michigan bowhunter Jerry Beck was in New Mexico when he liver-hit a mule deer buck with 3 x 4 antlers. The shot was taken at 42 yards, and Jerry said the arrow appeared to be going low when he last saw it. However, the buck stumbled after turning and starting to walk away, an indication that the arrow did connect.

Jerry ran up to the spot and from there was able to watch the buck run downhill and finally drop dead. After falling, the muley continued rolling downhill, and as it tumbled, one antler point was broken off. Jerry said it was a good thing he was in position to watch the buck, because there was a poor blood trail on the rocks as it ran.

It was snowing heavily when Robert McGregor saw a huge white-tail buck that later proved to have a typical rack qualifying for the Boone and Crockett Club's records. He got two shots with his .30-06 as the buck walked away. McGregor directed his partner, Gary Berger, to where he'd last seen the buck, and Gary found a spot of blood and some hair where the deer had fallen in the fresh snow. They started following the buck right away because of concern about snow covering the tracks.

They jumped the deer after only going 100 yards, and Gary took a snap shot but missed. The pair followed the whitetail until it crossed a logging road, then left the trail to have supper. They returned with a Coleman lantern to continue after the buck in the dark, hoping he would be dead by then—but he wasn't. The men heard the deer ahead but never saw it. The deer bedded frequently and left plenty of blood in the beds, but it didn't leave much blood sign while on its feet.

By the time the hunters pushed the buck across another logging road, it had quit snowing, so they left the trail there and returned the next morning. The buck was dead 100 yards from that road. Both of Bob's bullets had hit the deer, but one had only damaged muscle; the other had angled forward, lodging in the liver. Gary guessed the buck had covered between 1½ and 2 miles as a result of being pushed. If the heavy snow hadn't forced the men to follow so soon, and if they had waited until the next morning, that buck would have died near where it had been shot.

Bowhunter Jim Butler found himself in a similar situation after arrowing a 10-point buck. It started to snow, so he had to track the whitetail sooner than he would have liked to. He suspected it was hit through the liver. He started after the buck in the dark, carrying a lantern. Jim found five or six beds the whitetail had lain in before he started following it. After he jumped the deer, it stayed on its feet, stopping occasionally.

Jim pushed the deer until it simply couldn't go any farther, and he came upon it leaning against a cedar tree. It's illegal to carry a gun or bow in the woods after dark, so Jim had only a knife with him. To kill the buck, he cut a pole and tied his knife to one end, making a spear. At first, he tried throwing the spear at the deer, but missed. He retrieved the spear and slowly moved in close enough to stab the buck through the heart.

That whitetail was tracked about a half mile before it was recovered. Jim told me he had used a homemade spear to secure another liver-hit buck four years earlier. For another unique technique of subduing a wounded deer after dark, refer to chapter 11 on leg hits.

One fall I wanted to try taking a whitetail with a .50 caliber musket shooting maxi-balls. I finally got a shot at a spike buck, aiming for the lungs, as he walked by me. When the smoke cleared, he was on the ground but his head was up. Assuming the shot had broken his back, I hastily tried to reload to shoot again. But before I could seat another maxi-ball on the 100-grain powder charge, the buck jumped up and took off with his tail waving in the air, which wounded whitetails are not supposed to do.

The deer's back obviously wasn't broken. There was dark red blood where the buck had fallen, but none where he'd run off—and there was snow, making blood easy to see. I figured my shot had hit farther back than intended, due to the buck's forward motion and the split-second delay between aim and hammerfall. Maybe I'd caught the liver or the guts.

I was hunting that day with my uncle George, so I went to get him for help. About 30 minutes went by before we started tracking. The deer was bedded approximately 100 yards away, and we heard him run off but didn't spot him. Some 150 yards farther on, I saw the buck get up from its second bed; I took a shot but missed.

At that point, we decided to wait two hours before continuing. Judging from the short distance the buck was traveling between beds and the fact that it had let me get close enough for a shot, we were sure the buck was hurting. We also found more dark red blood, some of it mixed with stomach contents, confirming a liver/paunch wound.

In the meantime, I exchanged my musket for a centerfire .30-06, a more efficient gun for finishing a wounded deer. This switch wouldn't have been possible during a blackpowder-only season, of course. The buck bedded for a third time 100 yards from where we'd left his trail; he was weak but still able to get up and go. He bumped into a tree after starting off, an indication he was losing coordination. I got an open shot seconds later, putting him down for keeps.

Deer shot through the liver with sharp broadheads often leave a better blood trail than those wounded by bullets or slugs, even when there's no exit hole. For example, Ohio resident Ann Clark was bowhunting in Michigan when she arrowed a doe. The Terminator broadhead didn't go all the way through the animal but did slice completely through one lobe of the liver.

She shot the deer at 10:15 A.M., but she waited a couple of hours before starting to track with other members of her party. There was no snow, but she was using a Game Tracker string on her arrow. The string and lots of blood made the trail twice as easy to follow. The wound was on the right side, and a steady spray of blood went off to that side as the animal ran.

It ran about 300 yards and then made a small circle—at which

Ann Clark poses with a doe she bagged with a liver hit.

point the line broke—before dying. The dead deer lay within sight of the line's end.

Wounded deer sometimes backtrack over ground they've already covered before going off in a different direction. It's easiest to detect this trick on deer that bleed from only one side. Two separate blood trails next to each other will be visible where a deer has retraced its steps.

There are no inflexible rules in this business of tracking wounded deer, and that applies to blood trails from bow-shots that connect on the liver. A New York bowhunter watched a small whitetail he'd liver-shot bed down within 50 feet of where it was hit. It was getting dark, so the hunter climbed down from his tree stand and approached the injured deer. Predictably, the animal ran off, and there wasn't enough of a blood trail for the man to follow.

A tracking dog was used to locate that deer. It ran half a mile, lay down, and died. Knowing the whitetail was still alive, the hunter in that case should have remained quiet in his stand and tried to shoot it again, or left quietly to return later.

I've hit only one deer through a kidney, and that was an accident—as a hit in these small organs usually is. The kidneys are located just in front of the hindquarters below the spine. No one should intentionally try for a deer's kidneys, because of their small size. If a deer is hit too far back, however, hunters can hope their bullet or broadhead hits a kidney rather than the guts, as my arrow did.

I released the arrow at a small deer that was uphill from me. It moved as I shot, causing the shaft to connect in front of the hams. The whitetail disappeared over the top of the hill. Fearing the worst, I waited about two hours before starting after the deer. I was surprised to find a trail of heavy, bright red blood, and the deer lay dead no more than 50 yards from where I'd shot.

A shot that catches the kidney also has the potential of cutting the aortic artery and/or severing the spine. Deer seldom go far when hit there.

9

Paunch and Gut Shots

Hunters have an excellent chance of recovering deer shot through the stomach or intestines—if they go about it right. I've got plenty of examples to prove it. On November 6, 1987, while on an evening bowhunt, I gut-shot a spikehorn. For 5 to 10 minutes, I had watched the buck feeding at a distance of 10 to 15 yards. Because the buck was facing me most of the time, if offered a poor shot.

Finally, the deer turned broadside and I took the shot. But it moved ahead as I released, so the arrow hit far back in the body. The whitetail kicked out with its hind legs and trotted off 60 to 70 yards before stopping. The deer's gait was awkward and it looked hunched up when it stopped, typical of an animal shot through the guts.

If I had been hunting with a rifle or a shotgun, there would have been plenty of time to shoot the buck again, probably eliminating the need to track it. But there was no chance for another bow shot. I remained quiet to avoid spooking the deer. It didn't appear unduly alarmed, and I was confident that it wouldn't go far before lying down.

After standing for a few minutes, the buck walked off slowly, a sign that it was seriously hurt. One of the white feathers from my arrow was visible among the leaves on the ground where the deer had been standing, so I was confident of a pass-through, but I waited until full dark (about 15 minutes) before climbing down from my tree stand

Gut-shot deer can be recovered if hunters go about it right. A hit anywhere in the rear half of a deer's body often results in a paunch/gut shot *(within circle area)*.

to examine it. I did so as quietly as possible on the chance that the buck hadn't gone much beyond where I'd last seen it before it bedded. A coating of green slime on the shaft confirmed that it had passed through the intestines. Also, there were white belly hairs on the broadhead and on the ground.

The sky was clear, no precipitation was forecast, and the temperature was cold, so I decided to wait until the next morning to track the buck. I felt he would be dead by then. In the morning I found a steady, heavy blood trail. The buck had walked only 50 to 60 yards before lying down. He didn't stay there, however.

There was far less blood beyond the bed—a drop every five to ten feet for a while and then little at all. I didn't have to go far, though, before spotting the whitetail ahead of me. As he lay dead on his side, his white belly was visible for a long way through the open stand of hardwood trees.

The buck had traveled 250 to 300 yards from where he was hit and had bedded at least three times before dying. He had been dead for hours—no heat was left in the body cavity. Gut-shot deer tend to make a lot of beds, sometimes only a short distance apart, as they get up and shift positions.

In addition to the intestines, my arrow had sliced through the spleen before exiting through the belly. This accounted for the excellent blood trail initially. As often happens on gut shots, part of the intestines plugged the exit wound, causing diminished blood flow after the deer left its first bed. This is one reason you should not push deer with this type of wound unless it's necessary. Snow somewhat reduces the risk of pushing a gut-shot deer.

In some cases, entry and exit wounds from gut shots are plugged instantly. Once Dean Hulce was out with his brother Dale when Dale shot a small doe with a .54 caliber musket from a distance of 80 to 90 yards. Dean was standing off to the side, where no smoke from the shot obscured his vision. He saw the doe lurch forward when his brother fired and was confident he had scored a hit. But they found no blood or hair on the snow where the deer had been standing.

Bothered by the deer's reaction to the shot, Dean followed the tracks and found a pinhead-size speck of blood at the 100-yard mark. The deer was lying 50 yards farther on, and a second shot dispatched

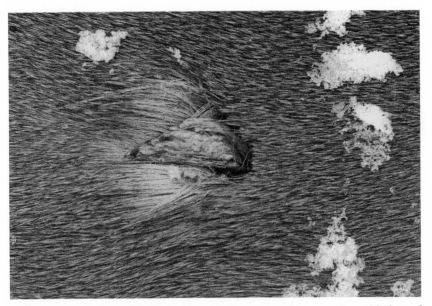

Both entry and exit wounds from gut shots have a tendency to plug with fat and intestines, reducing or eliminating external bleeding.

Particles of food and intestinal contents on this arrow confirm a gut shot.

it. Since intestines had completely plugged the wounds, there was no external bleeding. Convinced there had to be hair where the doe was hit, Dean went back and looked again, but he still didn't find any. So hair may not always be visible at the site of a hit. This example also illustrates the importance of following up on all deer shot at, even if there is no immediate sign of a hit.

Bowhunters can almost always tell if they've made a paunch or gut shot by examining the arrow. Green or brown particles of food will usually be visible on arrows that go through the paunch, and a much finer, slimy substance coats shafts that pierce intestines. If you suspect a gut shot but don't see these signs, smell the shaft. A strong odor clings to arrows that pass through the guts. There may not be any blood on the arrow—there wasn't on the arrow with which I shot the spike last fall.

Green or brown stomach or intestinal contents may be mixed with blood or found by themselves on the ground. Blood may be dark, but it can also be bright red. I gut-shot a doe that "jumped the string" (flinched at the sound of the string being released). The arrow angled forward through muscle on a hind leg before going through the large intestine. Much of the blood sign came from muscles and was bright red.

My arrow appeared to hit farther back than it did, and I thought it might have cut the femoral artery in the hind leg. I took the shot at 5:00 P.M. Waiting until after dark, my partner and I started tracking the whitetail at 6:30 with flashlights. There was snow, so I wasn't worried about losing the deer if we jumped it.

From both entry and exit wounds, there was a steady blood trail, but blood was dripping straight down rather than spraying to the side, indicating that my arrow had missed major blood vessels. But there was enough blood to suggest that the deer might bleed to death. We found the first bed after following the doe about 150 yards; the second bed was 25 yards farther. The animal had moved from those beds on her own. We jumped the deer from a third bed 100 yards farther along.

Convinced of a gut shot at that point, I left the area and returned the next morning with my brother. There was a clear sky and temperatures were cold, so the blood trail would still be visible and the meat wouldn't spoil.

We found the doe dead about 300 yards from where I'd stopped the night before. The carcass was stiff, but the body cavity retained some heat. There were nine closely spaced beds along the last 100 yards of the trail.

Whenever you trail a seriously injured deer and encounter multiple beds close together, look carefully for the animal ahead and off to the sides. It probably won't be far away. If the animal is still alive and you spot it before it spots you, you may have a chance to shoot it again.

I gut-shot one other deer with bow and arrow, and I managed to sneak up on it in a bed to finish it. This was another spike buck. The hit wasn't a typical gut shot. Since I thought the buck was closer than he really was, my arrow hit low. Connecting just above the line of white belly hair, the sharp broadhead sliced the belly open. Intestines started falling out of the wound as the buck ran.

The yearling buck went only about 40 yards before stopping, so I nocked another arrow, even though the range was longer than I normally shoot with a bow. Unfortunately, the second arrow went over the buck's back. If I hadn't seen my first arrow hit and hadn't watched the deer after the shot, the appearance of the shaft might have made me assume the shot had done little damage. There was no blood on it, just fat. But the brown-tipped hairs that were on the snow were typical of those low on a whitetail's side, and there were steady drops of dark blood along the trail.

It was about 10:00 A.M. when I hit the buck. I waited two hours before starting to trail it, with my brother's help. The nature of the wound made me think the buck might weaken sooner than gut-shot deer normally would, but it didn't. It went to the edge of a swamp to bed down, about 250 yards from where I had last seen it. As Bruce and I approached the swamp, I noticed a raven calling in a tree ahead of us and to the left.

Ravens have excellent eyesight and are quick to find dead or dying deer. Hunters who lose the trail of a wounded animal should watch and listen for these birds and other scavengers—they can lead you to your deer. Other scavenging birds to look for, depending upon what part of the country you're in, are crows, vultures, magpies, and jays.

I commented to Bruce that the bird was probably above the bedded buck, and it was. The buck left ahead of us, but there was a lot of blood on the snow where it had stopped, which is what had attracted the raven.

We waited four more hours and then took up the trail again. About a quarter mile later, I came to a series of beds close together. Thirty yards ahead I spotted the deer lying down with its back to me and its ears up. There was brush all around it, so to insure proper arrow placement, before shooting I crept slowly and carefully to within ten yards of the deer.

That same year, my brother gut-shot a five-pointer with a .50 caliber muzzle-loading rifle. The presence of snow was a big benefit in this case because the deer didn't bleed much—which isn't unusual on hits involving round balls from blackpowder rifles.

The buck came up behind Bruce and caught him by surprise. It was only 20 feet away by the time he saw it, and when he started to raise the rifle, the deer took off. It stopped to look back at a distance of 50 yards, apparently unsure of the source of the movement. Bruce shot quickly, aiming for its right shoulder. Assuming that's where the shot connected, he reloaded and started after the buck right away. Hair on the snow confirmed a hit. If he had stopped to examine the hair, he might have realized his shot hadn't hit where he'd aimed.

The buck went about 200 yards and stood in one spot for a while. Then it walked a short distance and lay down. There was some blood where it had stood, but none before that or in the bed. Bruce hadn't seen the buck when it had jumped from that first bed. He'd tracked it at least a half mile beyond that bed by the time I caught up to him.

Based upon the distance the whitetail had traveled, plus the fact that there wasn't much external bleeding, we were now sure the shot hadn't hit the shoulder. But the buck's tracks were easy to distinguish from those of other deer. It was dragging its feet, and the hooves were splayed even though it was walking.

The hooves of deer are normally spread only when they are running. Wounded deer, however, frequently walk with hooves spread, enabling hunters to follow them in snow. The large size of this buck's feet also helped us to distinguish its prints from those of other deer.

We left the buck's trail for several hours, only to find a second bed later just beyond where we'd quit. Unfortunately, we jumped the buck from that bed before taking a break. It was almost dark when the buck's tracks led across a logging road, so we stopped there and returned the next day.

In the morning the sign told us that the buck had been on his feet for a long time after it had left the second bed. It had gone through a thick swamp where it should have lain down again but hadn't. We came across blood occasionally, confirming we were on the right deer.

Prospects of recovering that deer didn't seem high, but we decided to give it a few more hours. Bucks that aren't seriously hurt seldom bed down at all when being followed, and this one had lain down twice. And it was dragging its feet more than normal, another clue that it was hurting.

We finally found the buck dead a quarter mile from where we'd stopped the day before. It appeared that it had walked until it could walk no more and had died on its feet. Such behavior isn't unusual for mature bucks that are pushed such as that one was. Although the antlers weren't large, the deer was at least 2½ years old, maybe 3½. It had been dead a while because the body cavity was cool.

The lead ball had entered the right ham, not the shoulder, puncturing the paunch and nicking the liver as it angled forward. Because the buck had been angling away from Bruce when he shot, the chunk of lead didn't have to be off target much to the left to catch the hindquarter. If Bruce had known he was dealing with a gut-shot deer, he likely would have left it alone for four hours or more after jumping it from the first bed.

Persistence and the presence of snow enabled us to recover that buck about two miles from where it was shot.

Over the years, I've clearly seen how differences in size, age, and sex of deer can help determine how easily they are recovered. On a bowhunt I shared with a group of friends, for example, two does were gut-shot the same evening. One was an adult and the other a yearling (1½ years old). We waited until the next morning to trail both animals.

Both arrows were recovered, having passed completely through the animals, and both were coated with food particles from stomachs. The hunters remained quiet after shooting and snuck away from the area to minimize disturbance.

We tracked the adult doe first. There was a steady blood trail but not a lot of blood. We jumped the deer after we'd followed it 300 to 400

My brother Bruce with five-point buck he gut-shot with a musket. We recovered it after a long tracking job in the snow because the deer was pushed.

yards. Then, not wanting to push it too far, we left that doe since there was no snow.

The yearling doe traveled only about 150 yards and died where it had lain down. Later that day, we located the adult deer, then too weak to stand up, in a bed no more than 100 yards from where we'd jumped it. Another arrow ended that tracking effort.

A 13-year-old cousin of mine bagged his first deer with bow and arrow while hunting with me during December. The deer was a six-month-old doe. As might be expected, Craig was excited when he notified me of his success, and he wanted to go after the deer right away, even though he suspected a gut shot.

An inspection of the site revealed stomach contents on the snow, along with dark blood and hair. Craig had missed a shot at a forkhorn before shooting the doe. We searched for and found that arrow and talked about the events of the morning to delay tracking the arrowed deer as long as possible.

After about 30 minutes, Craig couldn't wait any longer, so I agreed to track the doe with him as long as he understood that we would have to proceed slowly and quietly. If we jumped the deer without getting another shot, we would quit there and return later. The doe was bedded under a fallen tree on top of a knoll only about 80 yards from where it had been hit, and Craig was able to shoot it again before it got up.

This example and the previous one indicate that it may not be necessary to wait as long before trailing young deer that are gut-shot as it is for adults.

A wait of at least four hours is recommended before starting to trail an adult deer that is gut-shot. But if heavy rain or snow might wash away or cover up a blood trail, it's best to track the deer slowly just as though you were still-hunting. The objective is to spot the deer before it spots you. Gun hunters who are successful in doing so stand an excellent chance of getting another shot. Bowhunters may be able to do the same, but if they spot the animal and can't shoot, it may be best to remain there and watch rather than risk getting closer and spooking it.

Young deer will often weaken from poor hits sooner than adult deer, and sometimes can be tracked sooner, too. Here Craig Smith tags a young gut-shot doe that we tracked after waiting 30 minutes.

Mark Eby was hunting with a rifle when he gut-shot a spikehorn. Since the deer turned to run as he shot, he made a poor hit. There was about an inch of snow on the ground at the time, and more was falling, so he and his brother started tracking the buck right away. Mark told his brother there would be no talking. Any communication would be done through hand signals.

The pair progressed so slowly that it took them 2½ hours to cover 600 yards. At that point Mark smelled a strong odor from the deer. After moving ahead 10 feet, he saw the buck stand up and walk slowly away, but he was unable to get a shot because of thick brush.

After waiting 15 minutes, Mark snuck ahead alone and didn't go far before spotting the deer bedded. He had an opening for a shot and took it. Mark said there were steady drops of blood along the buck's trail as well as occasional bits of intestinal matter.

Frank Chapin from New York recovered a gut-shot eight-point buck he'd arrowed in the rain by following it soon after it was hit. He waited about 20 minutes before following the buck, but he couldn't wait any longer due to the rain. Jumping the deer from five beds over the course of 1½ miles, he spent seven hours recovering that deer. There was a steady blood trail but not a lot of blood. A number of times during the trailing effort, he had to get down on his hands and knees to find specks of blood. That position often reveals sign that you would miss if you were standing. Finally, he came upon the buck in a stream bed and finished it there. Gut-shot deer often go to water, a fact hunters should keep in mind if they lose the trail of a deer with such a wound.

If at all possible, gun hunters should try to anchor a gut-shot deer with a follow-up shot as quickly as possible—thereby eliminating the need to track a wounded animal. Paul Hannuksela did that very thing during December of 1987 while hunting with a musket. He was sneaking along through a swamp when he spotted a doe bedded 70 yards away and took a shot. As he reloaded, he was aware of the deer thrashing around. When he was ready to fire another round, he looked up and she was gone. He headed over and saw her in a hunched-up position as she was loping away across a clearcut. Concerned about being able to follow her due to a lack of snow, Paul ran after her.

Paul does a lot of running, skiing, and bicycling, and his good physical condition paid off that day. Despite heavy clothing and boots, he hurdled brushpiles and gained on the injured doe until he was able to shoot her again at 50 yards. He thus avoided a potentially difficult tracking job.

10

Trail of a Record Buck

One of the most remarkable efforts to recover a gut-shot deer involved a huge whitetail buck arrowed on September 27, 1986, by Curt Van Lith of Maple Lake, Minnesota. The persistence and skill exhibited by Curt and his relatives were exceptional.

That buck was tremendous in both body and antlers. It had a dressed weight of 264 pounds and a huge typical 10-point rack and ranks as one of the highest-scoring bow kills taken anywhere in North America. At this writing, the antlers are recognized as a Minnesota state record, with a Pope and Young Club score of 197 6/8.

There are a number of lessons to be learned from the story of how this buck was recovered. First and foremost is that an exhaustive effort will turn up most wounded deer. Hunters should view every deer they shoot at as a record-book animal. And each deer you recover and tag should go into your own personal record book, even if it doesn't qualify for state or national records. A large measure of personal satisfaction should accompany the successful recovery of any wounded deer, doe or buck, large or small.

Curt and his partners employed some interesting techniques to unravel this buck's trail. Some of them may prove useful to you the next time you must trail a wounded deer. The buck pulled some tricky maneuvers that others are sure to employ to confuse trackers. This case

Curt Van Lith with his record-book buck. *Photo by Curt Van Lith.*

is another excellent example of how stamina and the will to live enable large deer to go farther than normal, requiring extra effort to locate them.

Curt was hunting specifically for this buck. He had seen it a number of times, and a couple of his relatives had taken shots at it during previous gun seasons. He finally hit the buck at 6:45 P.M. during late September. It was a 42-yard shot, and the big whitetail was walking, causing the arrow to hit in the hindquarters—although Curt didn't know that at the time.

The buck hunched up when the arrow connected, typical behavior for a paunch-shot deer. But Curt didn't see the arrow strike. His sight pin was aligned on the chest cavity when he released, so he expected to get the lungs. The arrow actually entered in front of the right hindquarter, went through the intestines, and exited the left hindquarter. The buck entered a patch of woods and made a lot of noise, so Curt hoped it had gone down.

After the noise subsided, Curt climbed down from his tree stand and went to his truck to exchange his bow for a flashlight since it would be dark soon. He met an uncle, whom he asked to send help. While waiting for help to arrive, he looked for his arrow but never found it. The shaft may have stayed in the deer or been buried in the grass beyond where the buck had been standing. If Curt had found his arrow, he may have been able to determine from the start what type of hit he had.

Seven people arrived to help track the buck—more than necessary. Too many people can cause problems if they are disorganized. If they get ahead of the others, inexperienced trackers can unknowingly eliminate important sign. Realizing the potential for trouble, Curt took charge and gave specific instructions to his helpers to make sure no one got too anxious.

About 45 minutes elapsed from the time the deer was shot until they started following it. Fifteen yards from where Curt's arrow had connected, they found blood, and the flow got heavier as they went along. The blood was bright red from the muscle wound.

Where the buck stopped and stood a couple of times, it left pools of blood from a steady flow. All of the blood was on the left side where the arrow had sliced through hindquarter muscle.

Leaving the woods, the buck crossed an open meadow and a small township road that bordered the meadow (see the accompanying map that Curt provided). After crossing the road, the deer fell in a ditch on the far side, a sign that it was weakening. The whitetail fell again in a soybean field beyond, and blood was splattered in all directions.

"We thought the tracking was going to end soon," Curt related. "But we got an awful surprise. The blood trail disappeared, and the buck slipped into a cornfield, where it left big tracks and a smear of blood on cornstalks. We tracked him up and down the corn rows for over an hour. By this time I was pretty sure it wasn't a lung shot. We'd tracked him for a mile, and the buck hadn't lain down once."

Despite the lack of blood on the ground, the buck's tracks were big enough and the ground soft enough that the trackers were able to

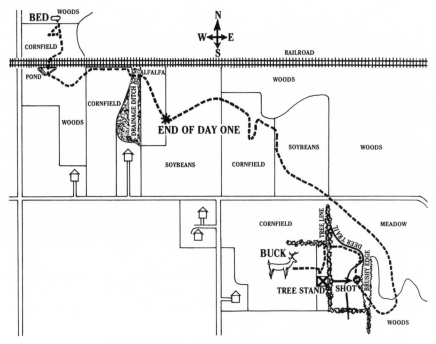

Course taken by Curt Van Lith's record buck.

follow fairly well. Going on tracks alone, they tracked him across another soybean field. When the buck entered an alfalfa field farther on, the group decided to call it quits. It was midnight by then, and the buck seemed to be still going strong.

Curt resumed tracking the next morning, but he admits his outlook wasn't good. Nonetheless, he wasn't about to give up. Based upon the amount of blood the animal had lost, Curt was confident it was fatally wounded. During a sleepless night, he convinced himself that he would find the buck.

Curt's brother-in-law Rob and his cousin Joe joined him on Day Two. It was slow going across the alfalfa field. Curt searched for sign while Rob and Joe brought up the rear and carefully marked each new find. In several places, all they had to go on were skid marks, bent alfalfa, and chunks of mud that fell from the buck's hooves. Since the buck had run across the field, it had left minimal sign. Eventually, the hunters reached the far side of the field and found where the deer had entered a brush-filled ditch and had slowed to a walk. There they were rewarded by renewed bleeding.

Curt's brother Scott joined the trio at that point. They found a chunk of fat on the ground near where the blood trail started again. The fat may have been plugging the wound, thus preventing blood from reaching the ground.

After leaving the drainage ditch, the buck had skirted a cornfield, then had gone through a woven fence into a woods that serves as a horse pasture. When they came to the pasture, Curt sent Scott and Joe around to the far side since he hoped they might jump the buck there. But the buck's trail ended at a pond on one edge of the woods bordering a set of railroad tracks.

Now two more of Curt's relatives—brothers-in-law John and Mike—joined the search party.

"Trying to second-guess the buck, I figured he went into the woods instead of the water," Curt said. "We spread out and searched the woods, but we came up blank. Scott and Joe didn't see any deer leave the woods, either."

So they started checking other routes the buck might have taken. They ended up in a cornfield beyond the railroad tracks, where they relocated the buck's tracks and blood sign. Apparently, the whitetail had swum across the pond, crossed the tracks, and gone into the corn. Remember, gut-shot deer commonly go to water.

"By the looks of the buck's trail in the corn, he was getting weak," Curt stated. "He was staggering and leaving blood smeared on the stalks. The excitement began to grow. We knew we couldn't be too far behind him now. The buck was headed north toward a small, brushy woods. If we didn't find him in the corn, he had to be in the woods."

They found a bed 10 yards into the woods, but the buck had gotten up ahead of them. Few other deer would have gone that far before bedding. Although this big buck did get up and go, the signs indicated he had had a hard time of it. A 10-by-10-foot area was torn up from the deer's struggles.

Assuming the buck must have plunged ahead into the brush, the trackers proceeded in that direction. They spread out and combed the woods thoroughly but came up with nothing.

"He gave us the slip again," Curt explained. "To recheck everything, I went back to where he had bedded. Then I followed his trail backward to the corn. That's when I discovered he had doubled back on us and had gone back into the corn.

"My brother-in-law Mike and my brother Scott came back to join in the tracking once again. Mike went down to the far end of the cornfield to watch. Following tracks and blood, Scott and I started back into the corn. Cutting across the rows, the buck was leaving an obvious trail. In about six rows, I stopped and looked down a row. There he lay with his head high, watching us. He was so big he barely fit between the rows."

Two arrows from Curt's 60-pound-pull bow were required to finish the record-book buck.

"I can't explain how I felt," Curt commented. "I was so excited and happy that I hadn't given up on finding him—although there were moments when I never thought we would find him. We simply stood there in awe of the giant buck."

Curt had earned that whitetail. It was 11:30 A.M. when he finally got the deer, about 17 hours after hitting it. He had started tracking at 7:30 that morning, adding four hours to the five he had spent the night before. Sometimes it takes as much time and effort to recover a deer as it does to get a shot. But it's all a part of deer hunting.

11

Leg Hits

If a shot breaks two of a deer's legs, the deer should go down instantly. However, even with both front or hind legs broken, mule deer, whitetails, and blacktails can and will push or pull themselves ahead. So another shot is required to kill them. That second shot should be administered as quickly as possible.

On a recent hunt on Trout Run Development property near St. Marys, Pennsylvania, Alabama hunter Jim Barton, Jr., dropped a nice eight-point buck on a drive. The buck was moving when he shot, and it dropped instantly, falling behind some trees. When it didn't move from the spot, Jim assumed he'd made a lung shot. Rules of the hunt prohibited him from leaving his watch until the drive was over.

As the drivers approached Jim's position, however, the buck started pushing itself ahead. Jim shot the deer again to anchor it. When he reached the whitetail, he saw that his first shot had hit lower than expected, breaking both front legs.

Dean Hulce was bowhunting when he broke both front legs of a doe. The arrow's impact knocked the deer down, but she righted herself almost immediately and bulldozed out of sight before another shot was possible. Dean found bone chips and tallow, but little blood, where the deer was hit. Bone fragments are commonly found in association with leg hits. Unsure whether his arrow had broken one or

Deer hit in either the front or back legs are recoverable. However, expect a long tracking job if only one leg is broken. Shots that sever the Achilles tendon *(circled)* are deadly.

both legs, and not wanting to push the deer too far due to lack of blood and no snow, Dean waited until the next morning to trail the deer.

A black bear almost beat Dean and two partners to that deer. The next morning they saw bear tracks in the mud along the deer's trail. When they reached the doe, they found claw and teeth marks on the animal—the bruin had tried to kill it. Dean thinks their approach scared the bear away. A second arrow was required to finish the whitetail.

Though both front legs were broken, the doe went three-quarters of a mile from where it had been hit. Dean's arrow had gone through the brisket in addition to the legs; that accounted for the tallow on the shaft.

During a fall evening, Dean's father gut-shot a whitetail a short distance from where the bear almost got Dean's doe. He waited until the next morning to recover the deer, and a bear beat him to the carcass. When he found the deer, one hindquarter had been eaten and the remainder had been buried in mud and leaves.

A young cousin of mine got his first buck, a six-point, with a shot that broke the front and back legs on the same side. The deer had been facing him 110 yards away, and the 180-grain bullet, aimed at the chest, went low and to the right. My cousin shot twice more as the buck flopped on the ground, but those bullets missed entirely. Bone chips from the broken front leg damaged the lungs, and that's what killed the deer.

A shot that breaks a front and a rear leg on opposite sides of the body should be just as debilitating.

Whenever one or both hind legs are broken, there's a chance that the bullet, slug, or arrow will also sever a femoral artery. These major arteries are located on the inside of the bones of both hind legs, extending as far down as the gambrel, where the Achilles tendon attaches to the lower leg. If gun hunters break a hind leg on a deer that runs out of sight, they should follow as soon as possible. If the artery is cut, blood will be bright red and may spray off to the side.

Once, with a .30-06, my uncle George broke a hind leg on a yearling buck. The buck went down, but it got up and ran as George approached. There was plenty of blood, and George followed it right away, catching up to the deer within 200 yards and breaking its neck with a second shot.

George's son once cut the femoral artery on a big doe with an arrow. The broadhead didn't break the leg but came close to the femur. We waited about an hour before tracking that deer, and we found it dead within 80 yards of where it had been hit. Blood loss had been tremendous, and I'm sure she was dead within seconds.

If that arrow had missed the major artery, though, death wouldn't have come so quickly. There are other blood vessels about one-third the size of the femoral in the meaty portion of the hind leg, and if one of those had been cut, it might have taken an hour for the deer to bleed to death. By then, it would at least have been weak enough to easily shoot again.

An hour is a reasonable amount of time for bowhunters to wait before starting to trail a deer hit in a hind leg—weather permitting, of course. If the animal is still alive after that time, stay on the trail as long and as far as possible, to keep the wound bleeding and to prevent the deer from resting. If it's hurt badly enough, it will eventually weaken, enabling you to get another shot.

I participated in the trailing of a doe hit low in a hind leg with an arrow. The hunter had hit the deer in the morning and had tracked her an estimated 1½ miles, finding good blood most of the way. He had jumped the whitetail at that point and had left the trail there, marking it well with tissue paper so it could be easily relocated.

Four of us returned to finish tracking the doe. We took turns, two members of the group looking for blood while the other pair marked spots as they found them. When the going was slow, three members of the group looked for blood.

The doe made a circle back to where the four of us had started following her. She got within 30 yards of our vehicles before turning in to a cedar swamp. There wasn't much blood visible as we tracked the deer across the swamp, perhaps because the wet ground soaked it up. The ground was soft as well as wet, however, enabling us to follow her tracks there. She was going on three legs, not using the injured hind leg. Her hooves were spread when walking because her weight was distributed on three legs rather than four.

The deer went from the swamp into a marshy area without an overhead canopy but with plenty of brush and tag alders. We thought we heard her go out ahead of us at one point. Not long after that, blood became harder to find and it started to rain. Frankly, I was about ready to give up at that point, but one or two others weren't. Their enthusiasm kept me going. It was a good thing we did, because the hunter spotted the doe bedded ahead of us.

The doe had finally weakened enough that she could go no farther. Another arrow finished the episode.

That deer was trailed at least four miles, but it was recovered, and that's what is important. It is often necessary to track leg-hit deer for miles. Although pushing such deer is recommended, you usually need a steady blood trail to do so if snow isn't present. If there's a poor blood trail, it may be better to wait half a day or until the next morning to follow.

It isn't absolutely necessary to follow the deer constantly. In the preceding example, the hunter left the trail for a couple of hours to get help. The break gave the deer a chance to rest, but it never actually lay down again from the time the hunter left the trail until the four of us caught up to it.

This example also illustrates the value of having one or more partners to help on a tough tracking job. They keep each other motivated. When one person's eyes get tired from the strain of looking for blood, another can take over. By working together as a team, they increase their chances of finding the wounded deer. I doubt whether a single hunter would have tracked that doe as far as the four of us did, and he probably wouldn't have found it.

This trio of hunters teamed up to track and recover a doe that was hit in the muscle of a hind leg. The job would have been much more difficult for a lone hunter.

I have taken part in a couple of other long tracking efforts involving leg-hit deer. One of them took two days to complete. The leg had been broken with buckshot, and the fracture was below most of the muscle. Although there wasn't a lot of blood, snow enabled us to stay on the deer's tracks.

Some other hunters had wounded the whitetail. I encountered one of them tracking the deer in the evening. I'd heard no shots by dark, so I assumed he hadn't caught up to it. Curious about the whitetail's welfare, my brother and I checked on it the next morning and found where the other hunter had quit. Concerned that he wasn't going to continue following the deer, we did.

During the night it had crossed a creek and lain down in three separate beds. We jumped it from the fourth bed, and Bruce saw it but got no shot. I then continued after the doe myself while Bruce circled ahead to try to intercept it. The whitetail crossed and recrossed a creek. It stayed in the water and walked downstream at least twice, a trick wounded deer sometimes pull.

Whenever the deer had walked in the water, I followed along the bank until I found where it had left the creek; then I resumed tracking. The second time the doe did this, she lay down on the stream bank, but I was so intent on looking for tracks that I didn't see her until I was practically on top of her. She caught me by surprise when she jumped up. I took two running shots, but both missed.

I pushed her out of another bed a short time later. When she crossed a road, I left her trail to regroup with Bruce. We were joined by the party of hunters who had wounded the doe, and one of them took up her trail. He also got a shot at her before dark, but he missed.

The next day Bruce and I and the other hunters continued after the doe. We pushed it from a number of beds. Finally the deer led us to a gravel road where the going was easier, and it tried to get farther ahead of us. Realizing that the animal was going to stay on the road, I ran after it as fast as I could and finally saw it ahead of me. Dropping to one knee to steady my rifle, I shot twice, ending one of the longest tracking endeavors I've been on. There's no way to know for sure how far we tracked that doe, but it had to be eight to ten miles. I'm sure that deer was healthy enough to have survived if snow hadn't enabled us to stay on the trail.

It actually took me more than a week to get the other deer with a broken hind leg, although I tracked it on only two days. This doe, too, had been wounded by another hunter, and a hind leg was broken in about the same place as the one mentioned previously. I originally came across her tracks, which had a little blood in them, during early December. There was snow on the ground, and bow season was open.

The blood also attracted the attention of some coyotes. I came to a patch of trampled snow where the coyotes had caught the deer in the open and had tried, unsuccessfully, to bring her down. Perhaps I had chased the coyotes away—I had jumped the doe from a patch of cover just beyond the trampled snow. As she ran off, I saw she had a broken hind leg. I suspect the injury had been caused by a bullet during the November gun season.

At any rate, there wasn't much snow on the ground that day, and I soon lost the doe's tracks amid a maze of other deer tracks. A foot or more of snow had fallen by the time I visited the area again where I came across that doe's tracks once more. Small drops of blood were still visible, and there was enough snow for the broken lower leg to leave an indentation as it swung to the side. This sign made it possible for me to separate her tracks from those of other deer.

Glimpsing her ahead of me now and then, I tracked her most of the day. She eventually weakened enough to let me get close enough for a sure bow shot. When my arrow hit behind her shoulder, she fell over, an indication she was worn out. This was my first bow-killed deer.

An arrow that cuts the Achilles tendon can be a better hit than most hunters realize. As mentioned earlier, the femoral artery extends that far down into the leg, and if it is cut along with the tendon, your chance of recovering the deer is excellent.

My cousin Craig made such a hit on a button buck during December. Because his arrow was deflected by brush, it angled back that far. The deer trotted only about 50 yards and stood in one spot for a good five minutes before limping slowly out of sight. We waited a little over an hour before starting to track.

A pool of blood lay where the young buck had stood so long, and there was steady blood beyond that point. Fifty yards beyond was a bed, and we jumped the deer from a second bed within another 40 yards. As it ran off, we could see it wasn't using its right hind leg. It was obvious the deer was hurting because it lay down four more times in the next quarter mile. The distance between beds got progressively shorter the more we pushed the buck. Craig finally got close enough for another shot.

I don't think we tracked the deer over half a mile. Another bowhunter who made the same hit on a whitetail reported finding it dead after trailing it a quarter mile. There was a steady blood trail in that case, too.

The scenario for hits in the front leg or shoulder is similar to what has been discussed for hind leg injuries. Deer may bleed to death from a front leg wound above the knee, whether or not bones are broken; the injury is likely to weaken the animal, enabling a persistent tracker to get in a finishing shot. It isn't unusual to track a deer with a broken front leg for miles before getting a shot, especially if the leg is broken below the knee.

Big game hunting consultant Rich LaRocco broke a mule deer's front leg with a muzzleloader in Idaho and followed five miles before recovering it. The leg was broken just above the joint and didn't bleed much. He said the deer went uphill for two miles, then downhill. Most of the tracking was done in the snow, but the buck eventually dropped down below the snow level. The deer bedded often.

When he finally finished the muley, Rich didn't know where he

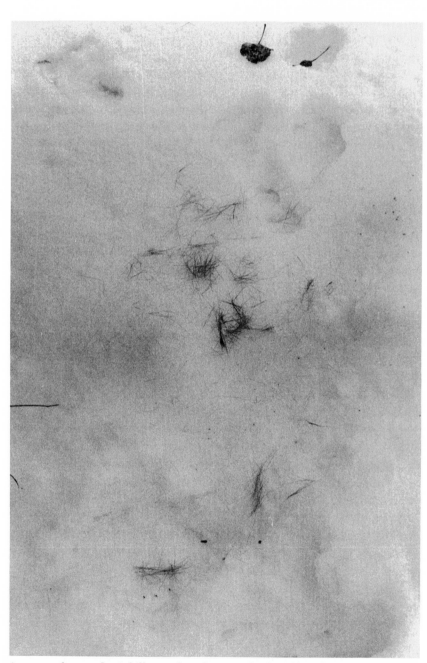

An arrow that cut the Achilles tendon of a young buck produced this hair. The buck was recovered.

Craig Smith examines blood sign from a deer with a cut Achilles tendon.

was, so he put an orange stocking cap on a bush to make sure he would be able to relocate the carcass. Some hunters neglect to do this and are unable to find their deer later. Mark the kill location with some bright item that can be seen from a distance, such as a hat, vest, sweatshirt, or gloves.

As I've mentioned a number of times in this book, young, small deer are usually easier to recover than adults, but this is not always true. Take, for example, the doe fawn that John Jeanneney tracked with a leashed dog on Long Island, New York. Its leg was broken just below the chest, and John said he doesn't think this deer weighed over 50 pounds.

Starting one evening and continuing the next morning, John and his dog followed this deer for over two miles in thick brush. There wasn't much blood. They caught up to the deer within half a mile the second day, but it jumped into the ocean and swam a quarter mile across a bay. Along the far shore, however, there was ice buildup that the small deer couldn't get through. The whitetail spent 20 minutes struggling before John reached it in a boat.

Jim Haveman helped a friend recover a buck with a broken front leg by lassoing it by the antlers after dark. The leg had been broken above the joint with an arrow, and tracking started about an hour later. The trackers might have waited longer, but rain was threatening.

The buck was jumped within 200 yards of where it had been hit. There was a steady blood trail but not a lot of blood leading to the bed. Once jumped, the deer started bleeding once more and went only 75 to 80 yards before lying down again.

In the light from his lantern, Jim saw the whitetail get up from its second bed. It traveled a short distance before bedding for the third time, a sign that it was weakening. Jim approached the deer in its fourth bed and tossed a rope over its antlers from a distance of eight or nine feet, then secured the rope around a tree. The deer expired in five minutes.

Dean Hulce released an arrow that sliced through the front leg on the far side of a big doe's body. The broadhead didn't break the bone, but there was a lot of blood. After following the deer a quarter mile before dark and about that far the next morning, Dean found her dead. He said there were eight beds in the last 100 yards.

Rob Keck, executive vice president of the National Wild Turkey Federation and an avid deer hunter, related an incident involving a big buck his father shot in Pennsylvania. The bullet went through the muscle of one front leg, through the brisket, and lodged in the other front leg. There was a lot of blood, and the buck bedded frequently, but it managed to stay ahead of them. The father-and-son team tracked the buck about four miles in the snow the day it was hit.

Returning the next day with two of Rob's uncles, they followed the deer five more miles. They were in mountainous terrain, and the buck always stayed at the same elevation. By the third day, bleeding had tapered off, but there was still enough blood for the Kecks to stay on the buck's trail. After they'd tracked the whitetail two more miles, another hunter finally shot it.

Losing a wounded deer to another hunter is always a possibility. Sometimes that is just as well, for the matter ends sooner than it otherwise would have. If another hunter kills the deer you are trailing

Always reload a muzzle-loading rifle after taking a shot at a deer, in case another shot is needed.

and the hunter is a sportsman, he or she should offer you the opportunity to tag it—unless the tag is already in place before the hunter realizes someone else is following the animal.

If the other hunter insists on claiming a deer you wounded, you should accept his claim graciously. After all, the animal was recovered, and that is the primary purpose of tracking a wounded deer.

Another buck wounded on a drive in the mountains of Pennsylvania was shot through a front leg. The shot broke the leg high and went into the brisket. Two hunters tracked the buck and were able to shoot at it a number of times but did not connect again. Finally, one of the hunters came upon the deer stretched out flat on a ridge. He thought the deer was dead.

Looking back at his partner, the guy hollered, "Here he is! He's not going anywhere."

But, when he looked back at the buck, he discovered that it was indeed going somewhere—and, in fact, was gone. If he had stayed quiet and had carefully watched the deer before committing himself, the hunter might have seen that another shot was necessary. After that deer ran off, a drive was planned for the area, and one of the watchers, encountering the wounded buck on the way to his stand, put it down.

Rich LaRocco and one of his partners violated the "always shoot again" rule while hunting with maxi-balls and muskets. After Rich's friend broke the hind leg of a muley, Rich found it bedded 150 yards from where it had been hit. He shot it in the neck but hit it too high. The mule deer jumped up, then put its head down on the ground. The hindquarters remained elevated but were quivering as though the animal was ready to topple over any second. So neither hunter reloaded his blackpowder rifle. The fact that the deer was able to stand at all should have been a tipoff that its neck hadn't been broken. Eventually they walked up to the muley, and it ran off. They had to track it two miles before getting it.

Sometimes the shoulder will be broken on a deer that is facing or angling away. This type of injury should be treated much the same as a front-leg hit in terms of recovery effort.

Montana outfitter and guide Russ Greenwood had one of his clients make such a hit on a buck at a time when there was no snow on the ground. The muley covered three miles before dark. The next morning, Russ posted the hunter at the mouth of a ravine where he expected the buck to go when jumped. He was right, and the hunter made good on his second chance at the buck. Whenever a deer has a broken leg or shoulder and is capable of covering miles before weakening, it's good planning to team up with at least one partner and to try to position someone where the animal might be intercepted while being pushed by a tracker.

12

Nonfatal Hits

It was the first week of November 1986, and Michigan deer hunter Randy Bruntjens was all set to bag the biggest buck of his hunting career with bow and arrow. The whitetail was feeding only 15 yards away. It wasn't in the best position for a shot, though, so Randy had plenty of time to watch it and count the antler points. There were nine.

After 10 to 15 minutes, the buck finally turned broadside and Randy took the shot. He saw his arrow—with a Razorback 5 broadhead at the end and propelled by a 60-pound-pull Bear Whitetail bow—hit high in the shoulder. The impact knocked the buck off its feet, but it got right back up and took off.

It was after dark by the time Randy, his brother, and a brother-in-law returned to look for the buck. They found no blood. The next morning, Bruntjens returned with reinforcements. They found the beginning of a blood trail 150 yards from where the deer had been hit, and they followed it until the blood petered out about a mile away.

Randy spent the next couple of days looking for a concentration of ravens or any other sign of where the injured whitetail may have gone. He was sure his arrow had killed the buck, and he felt bad about not being able to find it.

During November of 1987, Bruntjens was hunting from the same stand where he'd hit the nine-point, but this time he had a rifle in his hands. A doe approached, and she was followed by a big buck. The only shot Randy had was at the buck's neck. He took it, killing the 11-point on the spot.

When the meat from the deer was being processed, the butcher found a broadhead embedded in the buck's backbone. Randy recognized the broadhead—it was the same one he had hit the buck with the year before. Until then, he had no idea this was the same buck.

It was indeed the best buck of his hunting career. The whitetail, which had a dressed weight of 197 pounds, was 4½ or 5½ years old and was healthy. The broadhead was covered with scar tissue—the wound had healed perfectly.

Another Michigan bowhunter, Gene Ballew, has a similar story to tell. During December he took a broadside shot with a Savora-tipped arrow at a forkhorn. The buck was knocked flat, but it got back up and was gone in a matter of seconds. A determined trailing effort over two days failed to locate the buck.

During gun season the following fall, the same buck was killed by the father of one of Gene's friends who knew about the unrecovered

Broadhead lodged in the spine of a whitetail buck. The hit proved to be nonfatal, and the deer was bagged by another hunter the year after the injury.

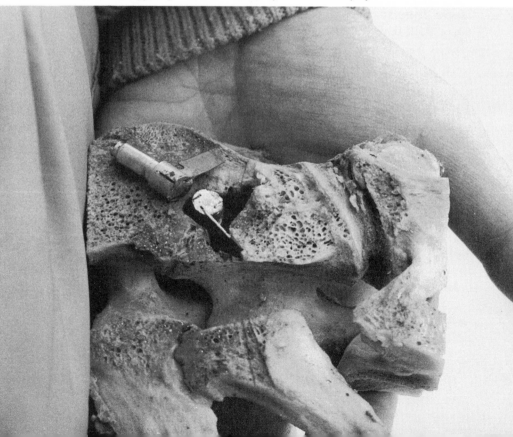

buck. The six-point buck was healthy. It was shot a mile from where Gene had hit it.

These incidents are two perfect examples of nonfatal hits by bow-hunters who thought their shots should have killed the deer. Such hits, especially with arrows, may be more common than many hunters realize. Clean cuts made by broadheads don't bring the shock, trauma, and tissue damage associated with gunshot wounds, and they have a greater chance of healing if blood loss is insufficient to kill the deer.

Because a higher percentage of bow-shot deer recover from wounds, and some are either seen or killed by other hunters, some observers conclude that the wounding loss (deer that die from wounds, but are not recovered) is higher during bow than gun seasons. Not so, according to Dr. Randy Davidson, research associate with the Southeastern Cooperative Wildlife Disease Study at the University of Georgia in Athens. Davidson, a deer hunter himself, has had the opportunity to examine whitetails that have recovered from hunter-inflicted wounds. He said that fewer deer survive gunshot wounds than arrow injuries, and so there are fewer of them to be seen than there are deer recovering from arrow-inflicted injuries.

A few years ago, a paper was presented by members of the Southeastern Cooperative Wildlife Disease Study Group, in cooperation with the University of Georgia's School of Veterinary Medicine, based on observation of injuries in a random sample of 1,002 whitetails. Seventy-six, or 7.6 percent, of those deer were found to have previous injuries from which they recovered. Ten deer recovered from head and neck wounds, 24 recovered from chest injuries, 10 from abdominal wounds, and the highest number (49) survived leg injuries. These figures add up to more than 76 because some deer survived multiple injuries.

The exact cause of most of the injuries was not determined, but 30 percent were known to have been caused by gun or bow. Pieces of lead, bullets, or broadheads were associated with 20 wounds that healed. These wounds were caused by buckshot (11 cases), .22 caliber rimfire bullets (3), centerfire rifle bullet fragments (2), birdshot (2), and broadheads (2). Of special interest is the fact that 25 percent of the injuries inflicted by gun and bow were probably the result of illegal activity rather than legal hunting. Deer hunters wouldn't be using either rimfire .22s or birdshot.

Nonetheless, this information confirms that deer do survive some wounds, regardless of how they are inflicted, and that their recuperative abilities are sometimes amazing. There was actually nothing surprising about the recovery of the bucks Randy Bruntjens and Gene

Ballew hit with arrows. Lodging in bone, the broadheads failed to sever the spine or aortic artery and missed all internal organs.

During January of 1987 I observed and photographed a healthy doe that had been hit with an arrow. The arrow was still attached to the broadhead. In most such cases, the shaft breaks or unscrews from the head soon after such a hit. This doe eventually lost the arrow sometime during the winter.

Healthy doe at a feeder, with nonfatal arrow wound high in the back. The arrow eventually fell out or broke off the same winter this photo was taken.

What is surprising is that some deer recover from lung injuries. Although this isn't likely when firearms are involved, there are documented cases of deer recovering from arrow wounds in which only one lung was punctured. If a broadhead damages a lung but misses the pulmonary vessels, the lung simply collapses and blood circulation to it is cut way down, reducing or eliminating blood loss.

John Jeanneney and some friends post-mortemed 51 deer at a location in New York where only bowhunting is permitted. A 101-pound, 1½-year-old doe had survived an injury to one lung the year before, and the lung was still functioning normally. There were scars obviously caused by an arrow in the chest wall and the lung.

Don Hickman from New York encountered another deer that had recovered from an arrow wound to one lung. This one was a healthy buck with a good rack. A broadhead and part of an arrow shaft were encased in the collapsed lung. Deer obviously can live with one good lung. This nonfatal injury was at least a year old.

In another example, a friend of mine is convinced that an arrow he sent at a 10-point buck penetrated the chest cavity, passing above the lungs and below the aortic artery. He was unable to find the animal after an exhaustive effort. At the shot, he thought he had hit the lungs, but he waited about an hour before starting to trail the animal.

He conspicuously marked blood spots with tissue paper. Finding no lung blood, he eventually lost the trail after covering a lot of ground. The buck never lay down, indicating it wasn't seriously hurt.

The person who owned the land my friend was hunting also owned an airplane. The two of them got in the plane and flew over the area in an effort to spot the deer dead or to determine where it might have gone. Although a plane is above and beyond the normal means available to hunters, it can be a good way to find a dead or dying deer in open terrain. Deer sometimes stretch out on their sides when they die, and their white belly hair can be easy to see from above. That's one reason scavenging birds frequently find dead deer quickly.

At any rate, the men didn't spot a carcass, but they could see the white tissue markers, which pointed toward a patch of heavy cover they guessed was the buck's destination. They were right. After landing, they went to the location and found more blood. The buck still hadn't bedded, though, and they ran out of blood again, finally giving up and figuring the buck would survive. I'm sure it did.

At the risk of repetition, I'll say that hunters should always try every means at their disposal to recover a deer they've hit. But sometimes, when the signs indicate the animal isn't seriously hurt and you've followed it far beyond what should have been necessary based on where you think it was hit, there's a good chance it will survive. A diminishing blood trail is typical of nonfatal hits, but this sign is far from infallible. Paunch or gut wounds have a tendency to become plugged. The end of a blood trail may also signal that an animal is running out of blood and is dead nearby. So don't give up too easily.

Dr. Randy Davidson examined a 4½-year-old doe—taken from the Pine Bluff Arsenal in Arkansas—that had a broadhead and six inches of arrow shaft in the chest cavity from an injury the year before. The shaft and head were completely encapsulated in scar tissue, and the deer was healthy.

In regard to gut wounds, Davidson said, "There is no question some deer shot in the paunch survive—probably a lot more than most hunters ever dream of—especially from an arrow wound, which is so clean. The biological reason is pretty simple: deer, like cows and sheep, have a protective outer lining around the paunch. That lining helps plug small holes poked through the intestines by rough, sharp forage the animals eat. This lining is a fibrous, netlike, lacy substance that looks like cheesecloth and covers most of the abdominal viscera."

Few hunters realize when they have shot deer that have recovered from gut shots, because they seldom examine the stomach and intestines. Even if they do so, careful inspection is required to see scar tissue from healed wounds. As mentioned earlier, 10 of 76 injuries to a sample of whitetails were to the abdomen. Only one of those healed injuries involved a superficial wound. The nine others were internal.

High back and neck hits that heal, and other superficial wounds, may not be noticed by hunters. Most noticeable are those on which a patch of hair is missing. Everyone generally accepts and understands that deer that are just grazed by a bullet, slug, or arrow will survive. Large clumps of hair, sometimes with skin attached, are typical of superficial hits. Although blood sign might appear heavy at first from such a wound, the flow eventually slows and stops. If a deer beds down, it does so as part of its normal activity pattern, not because of the wound.

I recently helped a bowhunter trail a buck he had arrowed in the neck. There was blood on only two vanes, with nothing on the third, a good indication the shaft had merely grazed the animal. Blood or tallow on only one side of the shaft itself also may indicate a near miss. There was a lot of blood at first from that neck wound, but it was dripping straight down rather than squirting to the sides as it would have if the jugular vein had been cut.

The buck was jumped from a bed after covering 200 to 300 yards, but it did a lot of wandering before lying down, stopping at regular intervals. An examination of brush where blood was pooled showed that the animal had been browsing. Seriously injured deer seldom feed before bedding. We found steady drops of blood after the deer was jumped, but they eventually petered out. That buck surely survived.

Besides superficial wounds, deer have the greatest chance of surviving leg injuries. Data from the Southeastern Cooperative Wildlife Disease Study confirms this fact, as do other observations. One spring, while turkey hunting, my partners and I saw three different deer with healed broken legs—they had survived the winter as well as the previous hunting season.

It's worth noting here that not all injuries deer suffer are caused by hunters. Collisions with automobiles account for some, as do "natural" accidents that deer are prone to (a specific example will be mentioned later).

As discussed in a previous chapter, deer with broken legs can be recovered, but they often have to be trailed for long distances. Sometimes such deer are taken by another hunter or a predator. I've shot several deer with broken legs that had been wounded by other hunters.

On the last day of the season one year, I shot a nine-point buck

Three-legged buck a year after being injured during hunting season. The animal was healthy and mobile despite the handicap. *Photo by Charles Alsheimer.*

that had a broken hind leg. The break was low and was well on the way to healing, so the injury had probably occurred about a month before, soon after hunting season opened. The buck was chasing a doe at the time I shot him.

Another time, I was still-hunting on Michigan's South Fox Island when I spotted a spikehorn and shot it. When I reached the fallen buck, I saw it had a broken front leg from a shot someone else had taken earlier in the season.

Fellow writer and photographer Charles Alsheimer of Bath, New York, photographed two whitetails with broken legs one year. One was a doe and the other a buck whose lower right front leg had been severed by a shot. Charlie photographed the buck during July and November the year after it had been wounded, and it was doing fine, although the deer's antler growth may have reflected the injury. The doe had broken her left rear leg in a fall on the ice during March and she was photographed during November.

The deer's ability to survive certain wounds should not reduce your willingness to trail an animal you've shot. Every effort should be made to track down each one of them. If you suspect the injury will enable a deer to travel a long distance, try to post other hunters in the area before starting to trail it, on the chance that one of them might get a shot. Or plan some drives in the animal's probable location.

13

String Trackers for Bowhunters

After more than one tough, time-consuming tracking job on a deer hit with an arrow, I've thought there's got to be a better way. In some cases, locating a critter lying a mere 100 yards from where it was hit took hours because there was little or no blood and other sign to follow. Most of the tough trails were unraveled through persistence and fine-tuned tracking skills, but luck played a major role on occasion.

Now there is a better way for bowhunters to trail and recover deer they arrow. String trackers can ease the tracking job considerably. There may be a number of these devices on the market, but the best model I've seen and tried is made by the Game Tracker Company.

The principle involved is simple: A free-flowing spool of string or line is fastened to the front of a bow, and one end of the line is attached to the hunting arrow. When the broadhead hits a whitetail, a blacktail, or a mule deer, the animal pulls the line off the spool as it runs, leaving a trail of string to follow. Sounds simple, and it is—if everything goes the way it's supposed to. However, one or more of the many variables involved in bowhunting can affect the outcome. Nonetheless, I believe string trackers are worth serious consideration by bowhunters.

The first time you are exposed to string trackers, you'll have lots of questions and concerns about them, as I did. Do they really work? Do

Bowhunter Gene Ballew in a tree stand with Game Tracker string attached to the front of his arrow, ready for a shot at a deer.

they affect the flight of arrows? What happens if the arrow goes all the way through the animal? I will try to answer these questions and others.

I was introduced to string trackers during the fall of 1979 when I obtained a Game Tracker to test. At first I was hesitant to mount the thing on my bow because I was skeptical about its performance. Then I watched a demonstration by sales representative George Gardner. It convinced me the device was worth a try. Gardner's arrows consistently flew straight and hit where he was aiming. The line streamed out so smoothly during each shot that string continued to unravel for a brief time after the arrow stopped. So I mounted the Tracker on my bow.

Most modern bows have holes drilled for attaching string trackers. The Game Tracker consists of a threaded bracket on which a plastic container is screwed. The spool of string goes into the container, and the line feeds through a hole in the cap, much like a fisherman's closed-face spinning reel.

The spool on that model held 1,440 feet of 22-pound-test line. Since then the manufacturer has come up with spools containing 2,500 feet of 17-pound-test line. That's a lot of string. Spools of Game Tracker line are now available in 30-pound-test, too, and the line comes in either white or orange. White line shows up much better for night trailing.

I made it a point to practice with the tracking aid as soon as it was mounted. I wanted to see if my sight pins had to be adjusted in any way to compensate for the string. They didn't. My arrows hit where I aimed, out to 30 yards, with the string attached as well as they did without. I seldom shoot beyond that distance, so I was satisfied. Archers who do a lot of hunting in open terrain where longer shots are common will have to adjust their sights if they decide to use a string tracker.

Before putting a new spool of string in its holder, pull some line out to make sure it comes off the spool as it is supposed to. On Game Trackers, the line feeds from the center of the spool. If it doesn't unravel smoothly, try rolling it between your hands or on a table while putting pressure on it. This helps loosen the tightly wound string so that it feeds easily.

With each new spool of line, I often take a practice shot or two at 10 yards to double check the flow off the spool. If it is a little tight initially, this helps loosen it.

String from the Tracker can be attached to a broadhead by unscrewing the head a couple of turns, wrapping the line inside the gap that is thus created, then screwing the head back down to hold the line. As added insurance, Gardner recommends securing the string to the shaft just above the head with tape. Electrical, masking, or Scotch tape works well.

The value of this advice was made clear on my first hunt with the device. Other members of the party were using the Tracker for the first time, too, and one of them arrowed a spikehorn. The string had been pinched between the hunter's broadhead and shaft, but no tape had been added. The head passed completely through the deer and was protruding from one side as the whitetail ran through tall grass. The broadhead unscrewed and the string pulled out after the animal had covered 75 to 100 yards. There was a little blood beyond the point where the string ended, but that quickly petered out.

What could have been a quick and easy tracking job turned into an affair taking up a long evening and part of the next morning. The buck was recovered by searching an area toward which it had been headed. The distance between where the string ended and the deer dropped was only about 100 yards, but there was no blood for at least 75 of those yards.

So a piece of tape can be an important item. Hunters who don't use screw-on heads will have to rely solely on tape to attach line to arrows. As an alternative, you can now buy wire rings that fit behind broadheads and hold tracking line.

String trackers are designed primarily for stand hunting. They can be used while still-hunting or stalking, but they aren't real practical for

Closeup of Game Tracker string attached to a wire loop screwed on behind the broadhead. The head in this photo is a Terminator double cut.

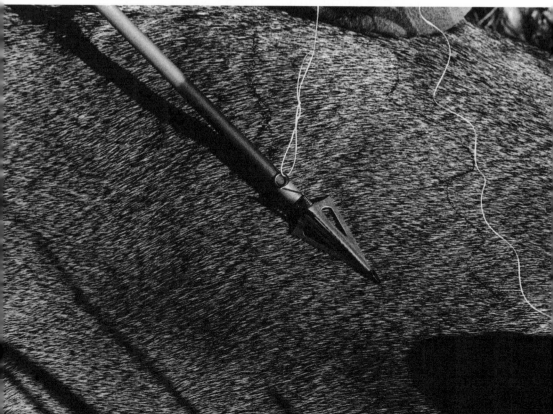

Lennie Rezmer shows a plastic container holding a spool of line mounted on the front of his bow, with line attached behind the broadhead.

those methods. If the string catches on brush or a branch as you walk, lots of line can unravel before you realize it.

For this reason, whether or not it's attached to an arrow in a quiver, line from a string tracker should not be allowed to hang free as you walk to and from a stand. To avoid problems with line paying out unnecessarily, I don't screw the spool holder onto its bracket until I'm in position, and I often take it off before I leave.

I've taken a number of deer with the help of the Game Tracker. On several, my arrow passed completely through the animals. When this happens, a double length of line—one end attached to the bow and the other to the arrow—leads to the deer.

In most cases, there has been enough blood so that I could have followed the deer without the string, but if the blood sign had been poor or nonexistent, the device would have been mighty valuable. That's what is so good about string trackers—they are a bowhunter's

I follow Game Tracker string to a spike buck I arrowed. *Photo by Bob McNally.*

the line for about a minute. Then, again, there was tension on the line and about five yards went out.

"After that there was no additional line movement. I surmised that the deer had made its initial run, stopped, and then moved around slightly before it died. My problem was that I was not certain just where I had hit the deer, as I had taken the shot as the deer had been moving past me and I had not been able to follow the flight of the arrow. If the shot was too far back, I did not want to push the deer too soon.

"I waited for an hour and a half before going after the deer. Upon returning to the spot where I had hit the deer, I found that the arrow had passed completely through the deer and had stuck in the ground on the opposite side, with the Game Tracker line passing through the deer. I have had this happen in the past, and you end up with that part of the line that passed through the deer being red and the other part being white. In this case, the rain had washed the line completely clean.

"I followed the line and found very little blood on the ground, as the rain had washed it all away. The tracker line led me right to the deer, but I would have had great difficulty in finding it without the line."

I never felt comfortable hunting in the rain with a bow before I started using a Game Tracker. In fact, I didn't do so at all, not wanting to take a chance on the water eliminating a blood trail. Rain isn't a major concern to me now.

Bowhunters who use string trackers should be sure to pick up after themselves. String lying around the woods is unsightly, like any other type of litter. On top of that, the line can be a hazard to birds and small mammals.

So that's the story on string trackers. They have advantages and disadvantages. Whether you use one is up to you.

14

Tracking with Dogs

The rate of recovery of deer shot by hunters would be much higher if the use of leashed dogs was more widely accepted and practiced than it is today. There is simply no comparison between the tracking abilities of hunters who use their eyes and dogs that use their noses. There doesn't have to be any visible clue of an injured deer's passing for a dog to scent-trail. When a blood trail is present but skimpy, with as much as 50 to 100 yards between drops, trained dogs can follow and find the deer in minutes while it might take a human tracker hours—if he reaches the end of the trail at all. Dogs can also track wounded deer easier than humans after rain or snow has fallen.

A New York State–based group called Deer Search, Inc., represents the only organized effort I'm aware of to use trained dogs on leashes to track wounded deer in situations where the hunters themselves failed. The organization is composed of dedicated individuals who are willing to volunteer their time for this good cause. Their unselfish efforts probably account for one of the highest recovery rates of wounded deer in North America.

As of late November 1987, over a span of eight years Deer Search volunteers had recovered approximately 300 whitetails that might not otherwise have been found. And the number of deer their dogs find annually is increasing as more hunters learn about their service and as

A New York State group called Deer Search, Inc., has increased the recovery of wounded deer with the use of trained dogs on leashes.

the number of people and dogs participating in the program increases. Both dogs and handlers have to meet stringent requirements before they become certified and are able to handle tracking jobs on their own.

Dogs have to prove their tracking ability on trails laid out by Deer Search members with blood collected from deer. These "artificial" blood trails are aged for 24 hours before dogs are started on them. Only dogs with the ability to follow such a trail to the end are certified. Handlers have to pass a written test and go through an apprenticeship under certified volunteers, actually handling a lead dog on six calls during the course of a year before they can be certified.

During the fall of 1987, in the Deer Search program there were 15 certified dogs and others in training. The organization included 52 members.

Deer Search services are made available to all hunters within the area they cover. There is no charge. Donations are accepted, however, and President Don Hickman of Pleasant Valley said that most hunters they help out, as well as local sportsmen's organizations, are more than willing to donate to the cause. Donations help cover volunteers' expenses while traveling to and from tracking calls.

Don said that when Deer Search was in its infancy and the concept of using dogs to trail wounded deer was not yet widely accepted, an opportunity arose to compare the ability of the group's dogs against those of experienced local hunters. He went to a local bowhunters' organization for support, and they were skeptical—many of them were expert trackers. Their response was, "It's a good idea, but we don't need you." So Don challenged them.

"Okay, guys," Don said, "let's have two of your people lay out a blood trail and we'll take two of our people and lay out a blood trail. Then you take two of your best trackers and we'll take one of our dogs and we'll see who finds the target. We'll let you go first and give you half an hour."

The experienced bowhunters failed to reach the end of the skimpy blood trail in the allotted time. When the trained dog took its turn, it completed the entire trail in about three minutes. The bowhunters were impressed. They've been strong supporters of the program ever since. So has anyone else who has seen Deer Search dogs work. Don said word-of-mouth among hunters has been a tremendous help in promoting the program.

Most of the dogs used in the New York search effort are German wirehaired dachshunds, and the best performers are females. These small, funny-looking pooches seldom fail to elicit a chuckle or at least curious looks among hunters who call Deer Search for help. Some hunters even express skepticism upon seeing the canines that are supposed to find their deer, but once they see them in action, their attitude quickly changes.

There are a number of advantages to using small dogs on leashes for tracking wounded deer. For one, it's easier for the handler to control dogs of that size. And if there's a question about the line a dog is following, it's a simple matter to pick up the animal and carry it back to the starting point. That would be impossible with a big dog. Small dogs are easier to care for, to feed, and to transport, too. When Deer Search officials were gathering support for their efforts, they discovered another big advantage of using small dogs: the public doesn't see small canines as a threat to deer. For that reason, the program was widely accepted.

Most of the dogs used in the Deer Search Program are German wirehaired dachshunds like this female, named Addy, owned by Don and Penny Hickman.

Larger breeds of dogs can be and have been used to blood-trail deer, and they pose no more of a threat to deer than the dachshunds do. The use of a leash at all times ensures that the dogs will always be under control. Other breeds used to track wounded deer include German wirehaired pointers, German shorthaired pointers, and beagles. Pioneer bowhunter Art Laha from Wisconsin used a female beagle to successfully track many whitetails wounded by hunters staying at a camp he maintained. German breeds are often the best blood trackers because they were bred for that purpose. Blood-tracking big game with dogs has been a longtime practice in Germany, and that's what inspired Deer Search members to promote wider use and acceptance of the concept in North America.

Not all of the whitetails Deer Search members seek with their dogs are recovered. Obviously, not all are mortally wounded—though the hunters may think they are. However, even in these cases, the service is valuable. A tracking effort is as successful if it results in knowledge that the injury wasn't serious and the deer will survive. The hunters can then rest easy, knowing the deer isn't dead.

The fact that many deer survive hits that hunters think are fatal points out two things. First of all, hunters aren't always able to accurately determine what type of hit they got. Second and more important, the reported wounding loss of deer (those shot and thought to be dead, but not recovered) is often inflated, especially among bowhunters. A clean, nonfatal cut inflicted by a broadhead heals quicker and more completely than a wound inflicted by a bullet or slug, which damages more tissue. It stands to reason that hunters are more likely to lose the trail of deer suffering nonfatal hits—not following far enough to confirm that the animals survived—than of deer that are mortally hit.

"When we talk to hunters, most of them are sure their deer is dead," said veteran Deer Search member John Jeanneney. "They are so sure that they don't want to bring along their bow or their gun. They say there was blood all over the place.

"On so many of these, the deer isn't hurt as bad as they think. We don't tell the hunter what we think about the wound while we're tracking the deer; we let him figure it out for himself. When the deer is jumping fences and still going strong 12 hours after it was hit, we ask, 'Well, what do you think?'"

Deer Search members discuss the situation with a hunter who wounded a deer.

I spent three days with Deer Search officers Don and Penny Hickman, accompanying them on four calls on which deer weren't recovered. In two of those cases, it was determined the animals weren't seriously hurt. One buck that was hit with a shotgun slug, for instance, was trailed both on the evening it was shot and again the next morning before it was decided the animal was unrecoverable. The second buck had been hit with an arrow. Both whitetails had lost little blood.

Another call involved a buck that crossed from New York into Connecticut, making it impossible to continue on its trail. It rained between the time that buck was hit and a dog got on the trail, but the canine followed the deer with no problem. Don has followed deer even after seven hours of rain and after two inches of snow have fallen.

The final call while I was there involved a buck with a broken front leg. More than 24 hours had elapsed since the whitetail was shot, and the weather was cold. Either the bleeding had stopped by then or another hunter had shot the deer where it had crossed into an apple orchard. The trail ended at the orchard.

Deer Search members prefer to get on the trail of deer with broken legs as soon as possible. Deer that are given the opportunity to stop and rest are often more difficult to recover because they usually regain strength, and because blood has a tendency to clot or freeze, closing the wound. Without any blood whatsoever, there is less scent for dogs to follow. Deer Search dogs are specifically trained to follow injured deer, reducing the chances of their tracking healthy animals or those that aren't bleeding. Countless times, Don has seen his best dog, a female named Addy, track a wounded deer across the fresh scent of healthy deer.

When they have been able to get on the trail soon enough, Addy and Don have been successful in recovering a number of deer with broken legs. One of those was a buck with a huge set of antlers that was shot on Long Island. A front leg was broken high up near the body. They followed that buck a good four miles over a span of six hours before they got close enough for the hunter to shoot again and finish it. The buck bedded six to eight times in that distance.

If a hunter carries a gun or bow while accompanying Deer Search members, the gun remains unloaded and broadheads stay in the quiver until the dog handler instructs the hunter to shoot. This procedure is followed for obvious safety reasons. Hunters can carry guns or bows on the trail of wounded deer only during legal shooting hours.

Don and Addy secured another buck on which the leg was broken only four inches above the hoof. Deer with that type of injury are normally difficult to recover. However, they were able to push this one fast and hard for three-fourths of a mile after they jumped it. The buck wasn't bleeding at the time it was jumped, but the wound reopened as the deer ran ahead of the trackers and continued to bleed.

The wounded buck went by another hunter in a tree stand, but the hunter was unable to get a shot at it. When the trackers went by, the hunter hollered, "Hey, you're only two minutes behind him!" They finally caught up to the whitetail after they'd covered a total of three miles, and the hunter finished it.

On a tracking job involving a deer with a broken hind leg, Don credits salt water for reopening the wound. This deer was shot on Long Island, and it swam a half mile across Long Island Sound. There was no blood when they jumped the whitetail, but Don found a set of three tracks, confirming they were on the right animal. The deer still wasn't bleeding when it entered the water, but when it hit the woods after its swim, bleeding resumed and it was heavy.

Don and Addy were given a ride across the Sound by a boatman who was collecting clams nearby and saw the deer swimming. The clammer knew what was happening because he had called upon Don several years earlier to track a deer he'd wounded. That deer went less than a mile from where it was shot to where it was recovered.

It isn't unusual for deer being tracked by a dog to go into water in an attempt to lose the pursuer. If the wound is in cold water long enough, bleeding sometimes stops, and there's little or no scent for a dog to follow thereafter. That happened to Don and John Jeanneney one time when a whitetail was wounded by a Deer Search member. The whitetail was running away when the man shot, and the deer half tumbled. There was an average blood trail, but not a large amount. Blood was smeared on brush at waist level, however, indicating a possible body hit.

Addy followed the deer 300 yards to where it entered a stream, but she couldn't progress any farther despite two hours of effort. A week later, the son of the hunter who had wounded the buck bagged it. It hadn't been hit in the body after all, but rather in the foot. Half of a rear hoof was missing. The hoof had been soaked in the water, stopping the bleeding, and that's why Addy was unable to follow the deer past the creek. On the early part of the trail, blood from the hoof had apparently wiped off on brush as the buck lifted its foot while running.

Gut-shot deer are often rated as the worst for hunters to recover because they can go a long way and often leave little blood to follow. The opposite is true, however, when dogs enter the picture. There's normally a lot of odor associated with the trail of a paunch-shot deer. That makes it easy for dogs to follow. Deer Search members have a high recovery rate of gut-shot whitetails.

Problems arise, however, when hunters push a gut-shot deer prematurely. Hunters who know they've hit a deer in the paunch should wait a minimum of six hours—overnight if possible—before attempting to follow it. Then, if they can't find it themselves, they can seek help.

If water is nearby, gut-shot deer tend to go to it, perhaps to drink or to cool themselves if feverish. John and Don followed a paunch-shot doe to a pond one time. Under some overhanging branches, she was trying to hide by lying in the water with just her nose sticking out. It took the trackers a while to spot her, but when they did, she was quickly dispatched.

With his dog, Hans Klein tracked a deer that was shot through the intestines. It had been hit by a bowhunter at 3:00 P.M., and the guys had watched the whitetail pull the arrow out before leaving the scene. Hans started on the trail at 7:00 A.M. the following morning and found the deer dead 600 to 800 yards away in a creek, where it had lain to cool off. Creek water kept the carcass cool, so the meat was in excellent shape.

Addy located a bow-shot buck 17 hours after it had been hit in the paunch with an arrow that went straight down through the back. Don and the dog came upon the deer bedded in a thicket about 500 yards from where it had been hit. It was still alive. Don instructed the young hunter to maneuver into position for another shot, but before he could do so, the buck got up and ran off. It went only 100 yards before going down again, however, and this time the archer administered a finishing shot.

Deer Search members also have a high rate of recovery of liver-hit whitetails. Hans recalls a memorable night-tracking job on which he recovered a 10-point buck that had been hit in the liver. (Volunteers are permitted to carry handguns when tracking after dark, both to finish animals and to protect their dogs. A few injured bucks have turned on dogs, and once a dachshund was pinned between a buck's antlers. Fortunately, none of the tines actually stabbed the dog.)

The 10-pointer was jumped after it had covered 300 yards, and Hans got a glimpse of it 100 yards farther on. Then the buck started falling, but Hans had left home in such a hurry that he forgot his gun. The deer got back up and moved off as man and dog approached. When the whitetail fell for the third time, Hans managed to sneak in

Don and Penny Hickman with Addy and a buck they helped recover.

behind it and put his foot on an antler, preventing it from getting up. The hunter then used his knife to kill the buck. That deer covered about 900 yards before they finally got it.

Liver-hit deer sometimes don't leave much of a blood trail and can go farther than most hunters realize, especially if only one of the side lobes is punctured. John Jeanneney participated in the search for such a buck, hit with a shotgun slug, which went more than a mile without being pushed before it went down. The last thing that buck did before collapsing was climb a steep hill. The trackers found only one drop of blood from that buck in a mile.

Sometimes it is difficult to determine exactly what killed recovered deer. John handled such a case while I was in New York. A big doe was involved. The sign indicated she had been hit high in the back—there was a lot of hair and smears of blood 30 inches above the ground. When he found the whitetail dead after going three-quarters of a mile, however, he saw that the slug had entered the front of the chest and traveled on the outside of the rib cage, failing to enter the body cavity at all. Such a wound wouldn't normally kill a deer, yet that one died.

John figured that the high blood smears were the result of the doe straddling brush and bending stems down under her. When the stems sprang back up, blood was visible higher than the wound actually was.

High back and neck hits are injuries that result in a low rate of recovery, according to experienced Deer Search members, because the animals aren't seriously hurt. In many such cases, by not shooting a second time, hunters are responsible for letting deer get away. Deer hit high are often stunned enough to fall down, but they are far from dead.

"Year after year, we get call after call about the deer that was on the ground and it got up and ran away," Don Hickman said. "In most cases, hunters could have easily shot them again. Unfortunately, when they see a deer go down, most hunters relax, satisfied they killed the deer.

"When we ask them why they didn't shoot again, they tell us, 'I didn't want to ruin any meat.' Then I ask them, 'How much meat do you have now?'"

It bears repeating: Always make sure a deer is dead before dropping your guard. If an animal struggles to get up, always shoot it again. Watch carefully as you approach. Look for breathing, evidenced by subtle movement of the sides. Also watch the eyes. If they are closed or moving, the animal is still alive. The eyes of a dead deer are open.

Don recalls one buck he recovered that was hit high in the neck with a shotgun. He came upon it in a bed in the daytime, about 400 yards from where it had been hit and 15 to 16 hours later. The deer was still alive, but its head hung down and it never attempted to stand up.

Hans Klein recovered a deer hit in the trachea with a slug. The hunter fired from a distance of 100 yards, and the whitetail dropped. When the hunter reached the deer, he took out his knife and enlarged the wound a bit, then started filling out his tag. As he did that, the deer got up and ran. Hans found the whitetail on its feet a quarter mile away and dispatched it with another shot—as the hunter should have done in the first place. The incision the hunter made with his knife obviously hadn't been deep enough to do any damage.

Deer Search members are able to follow up on most animals within 10 hours after they've been hit. But sometimes a full day elapses, and their dogs are still able to follow the deer. Penny Hickman used Addy one time to locate and recover a buck 36 hours after it had been shot. John Jeanneney used his dog to recover a Long Island deer

48 hours after the shot; tracking conditions were ideal, though, with no wind and high humidity.

Although the purpose of Deer Search is to help hunters recover wounded deer, volunteers want to make sure hunters themselves put forth enough effort to find their deer first. If hunters call shortly after making a hit and obviously haven't made a thorough search, they are often sent back to look farther or to mark the blood trail they followed. In many cases, a little encouragement and advice over the phone enables them to eventually find a deer on their own.

During my three-day visit with the Hickmans, there were two or three instances in which hunters who resumed the search after contacting the organization found their deer before a volunteer could respond. One of the whitetails was a 10-point buck.

Occasionally a deer is shot and tagged by another hunter before the first hunter or a Deer Search volunteer reaches it. Don told me that members have found gut piles at the end of about 30 blood trails. If a deer they are tracking is down but not tagged when they arrive, dog handlers remain neutral if there's a question about who should get the deer. However, it's generally accepted that whoever kills the deer gets to keep it.

For a different perspective on this subject, refer to the last chapter in this book.

Deer Search volunteers work closely with police and conservation officers. In all cases, local law-enforcement agencies and conservation officers are notified where and when Deer Search will be tracking. When private property is involved, permission is secured from the landowner.

The group is sometimes called upon to find animals shot illegally, and the dogs have done their job well in those instances. Dogs trained to track wounded deer can be very valuable to officers who enforce game laws.

How are dogs trained to track wounded deer? Some, especially those of German breeding, do it naturally, requiring only some encouragement and reinforcement to develop their ability. One way to do this is to take a dog on the blood trail of a deer you've already located, or on a heavy blood trail that is easy to follow. If and when it reaches the carcass, praise the dog and give it a reward.

As mentioned earlier, members of Deer Search collect blood from deer kills and use it to lay out training trails. Beef blood can also be used. A deer hide is usually placed at the end of the trail, and dogs are rewarded when they reach it.

Blood trails are usually placed so that the wind will be at a dog's back as it follows the scent. Markers are placed along the trail so the dog handler will know when and if a dog strays from the line. The blood trails are lengthened, "aged," and made more difficult as a dog's training progresses.

If you are interested in obtaining more information about tracking wounded deer with dogs, starting a chapter of Deer Search in your state, or making a contribution, write Deer Search, P.O. Box 853, Pleasant Valley, NY 12569. Don and Penny Hickman's phone number is 914/635-3641.

15

Mistaken Impressions

In tracking wounded deer, making assumptions can get you in trouble. Hunters should also expect the unexpected in order to broaden their perception of what a wounded deer might do. It isn't unusual for whitetails, blacktails, and mule deer to do the unexpected when hurt, pressured, and panicky. In their haste to locate wounded or dead deer, hunters sometimes see or hear things that lead them astray.

This happened to bowhunter Fred Becknell. He arrowed an eight-point buck in the chest when it was almost on top of him. The buck ran only about 20 yards, then lay down under a tree, and in a short time its head drooped to the ground.

Fred walked up to the whitetail. It looked dead, so he assumed it was. That was his first mistake. The archer put his bow down, took off his coat, and was taking his knife out when the buck suddenly raised his head, shook, blinked its eyes, jumped up, and took off.

When Fred followed after the buck, he heard a deer crash off to the north. He assumed his deer had lain down again and run off at his approach. Mistake No. 2.

All attempts to pick up the wounded whitetail's trail to the north failed. Frustrated, Fred enlisted the help of hunting partner John Driver. Unencumbered by assumptions, John checked out directions other than north and found a blood trail leading to the south. The deer

Becknell had heard wasn't the one he'd hit but rather a healthy one. The men located the chest-shot buck.

If you run into a dead end on the trail of a deer, consider all possible routes the animal could have taken. Start with the most likely options, but if they don't pan out, investigate unlikely ones. We humans can't fully comprehend a deer's behavior patterns, whether it is healthy or hurt. That's why it's important not to make assumptions based upon human perception.

Whitetails won't normally submerge themselves in water. However, John Jeanneney and Don Hickman tracked a doe one time that they found hiding underwater with just her nostrils above the surface. Would you have thought to look there?

You may have heard or read that seriously wounded deer don't go uphill. Most of them may not, but some of them do. So don't ignore that option. Hickman tracked one gut-shot whitetail that went up a steep hill. The buck got three-fourths of the way to the top before it ran out of steam. Don found the deer bedded and shot it again. That deer went a total of 700 to 800 yards.

An injured deer may make a sudden change in direction for no apparent reason, and this sometimes confuses a trailing hunter. It shouldn't cause too much of a delay, however, if you expect the unexpected and consider "impossible" routes.

Rich LaRocco told me that he may not have found a mule deer buck one of his clients shot if he hadn't seen it pull such a maneuver. The muley started toward some cover, but before reaching it, he changed directions and entered a different patch of brush. Because the deer was in the open and visible when it turned, they saw where it went and found it dead a short distance from where it went out of sight. If the muley had been on the edge of cover when shot, and had made the tricky turn after it had gone out of sight, the guide would have concentrated his search in the wrong area. This particular muley's trail would have been especially tough to unravel because there was no blood sign.

The eyes can be deceived, too. Sometimes we "see" things that don't actually happen. Consider veteran bowhunter George Gardner's experience. He arrowed a buck and then watched it run and fall dead. A friend who had never bowhunted before was with George that day, so George went to get his friend to show him how to track a deer. There was snow on the ground, making tracking easy.

George came to a dead end, however, during several attempts to follow the buck. He finally gave up on tracking and went to where he knew the deer had fallen. Once George reached the carcass, he backtracked the animal from there. In doing so, he discovered that the buck had started out in one direction but after running a short distance had pulled a 360 degree turn, going back the way it had come before going down.

George swore he'd seen that buck run in a continuous loop around him before falling. The end result was that George's friend learned a more valuable tracking lesson than George had planned. Hunters can learn a lot about the behavior of wounded deer by back-tracking animals they've shot.

If you fire at a deer that is with others, it can be difficult to keep an eye on the animal you've hit as they all scatter after the shot. You may even hit a different deer than the one you aimed at. There have been cases of two deer killed with one shot. So it is important to shoot only at animals that are isolated from others in a group, especially when using firearms. But be aware that multiple kills are possible with the bow, too.

Late one bow season a friend of mine was anxious to fill his tag. He sat in a ground blind watching a narrow strip of rye grass where deer had been grazing. A group of four or five animals fed toward him, and as they got within bow range, he concentrated all his attention on a decent-sized doe. That's the one he decided to take.

The doe was almost broadside when the bowman shot, and he saw his arrow enter behind her shoulder. All the deer ran at the shot.

In this situation it would be easy to get two deer with one shot, both bucks. Hunters should hold their fire until a deer is isolated from others. However, there have been cases in which two deer were shot when the hunter wasn't aware of the second deer's presence. This may have happened if you find two blood trails where there should be only one.

Bob Vincent *(left)* congratulates Sam Grissom on a spike buck they tracked and recovered in the dark. Bob Brandau is in the middle. Sam confused the buck with another deer as they ran off.

The doe he'd hit entered a thick patch of young aspen trees to his left, and he heard her fall twice. The archer was confident the deer was dead, but he decided to get help before following it. He sat in his blind for five or ten minutes, confirmed that there was a blood trail, and then went to get two hunting companions.

They returned with lights and determined that the doe was indeed dead and had gone only 40 yards before piling up. The trio had a surprise waiting for them, though, when they went looking for the hunter's spent shaft: there was a second blood trail.

They followed that one and found a second dead deer, the hunter's arrow buried behind its shoulder. The arrow had gone completely through the doe and into the smaller deer. The hunter was totally unaware of the second deer's presence until the trio found the second blood trail. The doe had obviously screened it from view. The shot had been taken with a 60-pound-pull compound bow.

As this example shows, it's easy to overlook the presence of a second deer when you are concentrating on taking a shot. You should be suspicious that two deer may have been hit with one shot if you find two blood trails, or if you follow and find an animal you are sure you didn't shoot at.

Even if only one deer in a group is hit, it's easy to get confused about which one is which as they run off—and to end up watching the wrong one. I'm sure that's what bowhunter Sam Grissom did one evening. There were six deer in front of him, and one was a spikehorn, which he shot. I returned after dark with Sam and two other hunters to

Craig Smith holds up the head of a doe he hit with an arrow intended for a deer standing behind this one.

track the deer. Sam said the buck had run straight away for a short distance, then swung to the left. A search along the deer's likely course failed to turn up anything. Realizing that Sam may have confused the deer he'd hit with others, I started looking elsewhere and found a blood trail going to the right.

From there, it was easy to find the deer. There was steady blood to where it had gone down. The buck ran about 150 yards after being hit through the lungs.

Another time, a cousin of mine hunting with me took a shot at a doe standing broadside. There were actually two does fairly close together. The one he aimed for was facing to the left. The other one was facing to the right and was a little closer than the target animal. The two bodies overlapped, with the rear of the closer doe covering part of the other doe's body. But my cousin could see the shoulder area of the farther doe. That's where he aimed and thought he had hit.

However, we found a blood trail going to the right rather than the left. The arrow had hit the closer deer in a hindquarter instead of the farther deer in the shoulder area. Fortunately, the broadhead cut a femoral artery. There was plenty of blood, and the doe went only 80 yards before dying.

Even when only one deer is involved, it's easy to hit somewhere other than where you think you did, with gun or bow. Two prime examples were discussed in earlier chapters. One case is in the chapter covering gut shots and involves a buck my brother shot with a musket. He thought he hit it behind the shoulder, but got the guts instead.

The other example is in chapter 10, which covers a record-book buck Curt Van Lith arrowed. He also thought he punctured lungs, but he pierced guts instead. In both cases, if the hunters had known where their shots had hit, they probably would have gone about trying to recover them differently and may have been able to do so with less effort.

With such examples in mind, do everything possible to confirm the location of a hit, wherever you think it may be. In doing so, consider hair, blood sign, and the deer's actions. Closely examining the sign and considering all options should help reduce the chances of mistaken impressions.

16

Another Hunter's Deer

On the second day of Michigan's gun deer season, my brother Bruce had barely entered the woods on the way to his stand when he encountered a blood trail. The blood, obviously left by a wounded whitetail, was easy to see on the crusted snow.

There was no evidence the hunter who had wounded the animal had followed it. Bruce decided to take the trail. He traveled only a short distance when he happened to look up, and there, not 30 yards away, lay the deer staring at him. It was a buck—a big one.

The sight of the many-tined, wide-racked buck at such close range caught my brother by surprise. It might have been that factor—plus uncertainty about how badly the buck was hurt—that made him react as he did. Whatever the reason, Bruce took three steps backward. The buck was on his feet and going away in a split second, giving Bruce time for one quick shot. The bullet missed. Bruce forgot all about sitting for the afternoon. He kept after the injured buck until he finally got him. The wide-racked nine-point had a broken hind leg and eventually got so weak from loss of blood that it could go no farther.

After the deer was dead, Bruce returned to the spot where he'd originally come across the blood trail, and he backtracked the deer for a while. There was still no sign of the hunter who had originally hit the whitetail. Apparently the shooter had long since given up on the deer, or didn't even know he had hit it. So Bruce tagged the animal.

This episode points up the importance of following a blood trail, whether the deer was hit by you or by another hunter. But before starting out on the trail of a deer hit by someone else, try to make sure the other hunter isn't already following the animal. Either follow the backtrack or wait about a half hour to see if anyone comes along. If not, trail away.

If you do start out on the trail of a deer wounded by someone else, be prepared to relinquish the animal if you bag it and he or she comes along. That is the ethical thing to do.

Why bother trailing a wounded deer that you may not be able to keep? I firmly believe that hunters have an ethical responsibility to the game they hunt. That responsibility includes not only striving for quick, clean kills but also finishing any wounded animal as quickly as possible, depending on the circumstances. This includes shooting any injured deer you come across. Hunters who accept this responsibility will feel good about themselves and their sport—even if someone else ends up tagging the deer. I say this from personal experience.

The day after my brother collected the nine-point, he and I and our uncle George went to another location where there was no snow. Bruce came along primarily to try to keep the deer moving, which would increase the chances that George and I might see whitetails from our stands in a thick cedar swamp.

About 9:00 A.M., four shots were fired close to my stand on top of a steep ridge that overlooked the swamp. Then I heard a boy holler, "Dad, c'mon over! It was a big one!"

I waited and listened to determine if the deer would come my way. It didn't, and after a while, I forgot about the incident. An hour and a half later, George and I were walking along the same ridge, just below the top, when I heard a racket on the opposite side. The source of the noise became apparent as soon as I reached the top of the ridge. A big-racked buck was racing toward me at almost point-blank range, and he was bleeding. The boy's earlier words flashed through my mind. The buck was so close, I don't think I even aimed. I pointed the barrel of my .30-06 at his shoulder and fired. The bullet struck home, but another round was required to put the buck down for keeps.

When the shooting was over, a voice called, "Who's there?" I thought at first that it was the boy or his father, but I was wrong. It was Bruce.

He had come across another blood trail in his wanderings and, as he had the day before, he had started following it when he saw no sign of anyone else around. Moments after he jumped the animal, he heard me shoot. What a coincidence—our party had taken two big bucks in

I hold up the head of an eight-point buck that was wounded by a 14-year-old boy. I finished it after my brother pushed it to me by following the blood trail. The boy tagged the deer.

two days, both deer that other hunters had wounded. This buck had an eight-point rack with long tines and fairly wide beams. The rack was more impressive than any worn by whitetail bucks I had collected previously.

I was pleased about bagging the buck, but I couldn't understand why the father and son would leave without following the blood trail. It wasn't long before I found out. We were taking photos of the deer when someone else came along the blood trail. It was one of the boy's uncles.

After the father and son realized the buck was hit, they left to get help, returning with two of the father's brothers. One of them took the trail while the others posted in the vicinity to try to intercept the deer once it was jumped. They obviously knew what they were doing and had no intention of leaving a wounded whitetail in the woods.

I learned that the boy was 14 years old. It was his first hunt and his first deer. My decision to let the boy tag the buck was an easy one to make. I was pleased to have played a part in the tagging of his first buck, especially such a nice one.

Besides being the right thing to do, my decision enabled me to continue hunting. And that's what I enjoy most about deer hunting—the pursuit, not the kill. The hours and days spent in anticipation of a shot—plus the many sights, sounds, and other experiences that enrich those hours and days—make that shot all the more valuable when, and if, it does come.

I eventually filled my tag with a nice 11-point buck. The tines weren't as long as those on the eight-point, but they were heavier, as were the beams. Which rack was the better? That's not important. I'm satisfied with the one I brought home. I look at it as my reward for being a sportsman.

A friend of mine had a similar experience. Toward evening of opening day, Mark Eby heard, then saw, a buck approach his stand. The whitetail was breathing heavily and limping badly. Mark shot the eight-point at a distance of 100 feet and went up to it, noting it had a broken front leg. There was snow on the ground, and a short time later, the hunter who had wounded the buck and followed its tracks arrived.

As the trailing hunter approached the fallen buck, Mark said, "As far as I'm concerned, this is your deer."

The guy was obviously grateful for Mark's attitude, but he had definitely earned the right to tag the whitetail. He had wounded the buck about noon and stayed on its trail 4½ hours. Mark figured the hunter had followed the buck about 2½ miles.

The tag Mark could have put on that wounded 8-point later went on a 10-pointer he collected on a drive.

New Yorker Don Hickman recovers a lot of wounded deer every fall for other hunters with his tracking dogs, but one time he got to tag a buck himself that had been shot by someone else. A sheriff saw the eight-point cross a road with an obvious broken hind leg and called Don. With his wife Penny, Don waited three hours by that crossing on the chance that the hunter might come along. When no one did, they tracked the whitetail, jumping it after going 300 yards. It entered a swampy area and finally stood fast to face the leashed dog that was approaching. At that point, Don dumped the deer with a slug.

I bagged this 11-point buck with a musket after letting the youngster tag the eight-point. Maybe it was my reward.

What should you do if you encounter a doe wounded by someone else and you are licensed to shoot only antlered bucks? A hunter's ethical responsibility to wounded deer does not supersede game laws. You should shoot only animals that are legal under your license. If a wounded doe passes your stand and your tag is for bucks only, you are obligated to hold your fire. The same obligation applies if you trail a deer wounded by someone else and discover it is a doe.

Leaving a wounded deer can be tough, but hunters who elect to do otherwise stand to face a stiff fine—regardless of how good their intentions are. Wardens hear countless stories from violators. Few admit they were intentionally breaking the law. Even if you do the ethical thing by finishing a wounded deer, you are still breaking the law if the animal isn't legal on your license.

However, there may be a way to be both ethical and legal. My advice to hunters who see wounded deer that aren't legal for them is to locate someone who has a valid permit and encourage him or her to pursue the injured animal. If that isn't possible and the deer is seriously hurt, try contacting a game warden. Handling such situations is part of a warden's job.

Keeping the above advice in mind, hunters who pick up the trail of a wounded deer they didn't hit should identify its sex before shooting at it. Some does end up wounded even in bucks-only areas, so don't assume that an injured deer is a buck until you confirm it by sight.

Once you do, and a shot is offered, try to be sure you're shooting at the right animal. Deer that are trailed frequently seek out other deer. Bruce and I learned this one firsthand while tracking a wounded deer years ago. The animal had been wounded by a hunter Bruce knew, and we were helping him secure it. We had covered quite a few miles when a deer appeared in front of us. Assuming it was the one we were after, Bruce shot without taking the time to look at the animal's head.

It turned out to be a doe, but fortunately for us, we had a valid tag to put on it. You might not be as lucky in a similar situation. We eventually caught up to the wounded deer and finished it.

Most of the discussion so far in this chapter has involved hunting with firearms. The chances of seeing a deer wounded by another hunter, or of seeing the trail of one, are greatest during gun seasons due to the large numbers of hunters afield. However, it can also happen during archery seasons, so this chapter's advice also applies to bowhunters (although deer of either sex are uniformly legal for bowhunters). The first whitetail I collected with bow and arrow had been wounded by someone else and was discussed in the chapter on leg hits.

On a more recent late-season bowhunt, two of us had the chance to recover a buck arrowed by another hunter. The guy had hit the deer the evening before, putting a broadhead down into the body cavity through the top of the back. After a wait of 1½ hours, he followed a

Paul Hannuksela kneels by a five-point buck we found the day after it had been shot by another hunter.

good blood trail on the snow in the dark, jumping the buck from a bed after an estimated half mile. There was no blood beyond the bed, and the guy gave up on the deer despite the fact that there was good tracking snow. He had to work the following day and couldn't return.

A friend of mine was hunting with this fellow and knew I would be in the same area the next day, so he called and told me the situation, giving me directions to where the buck had been hit.

It snowed overnight, but my partner and I could still see the blood trail left by the arrowed buck. It had actually bedded within 200 yards—not half a mile—of where it had been hit. The distance obviously had seemed longer in the dark.

From the hunter's efforts to locate the deer the previous evening, the snow was all tracked up near the bed, so it was impossible to sort out the buck's tracks. The two of us simply headed in the direction we thought the deer should have gone. We soon found it 150 yards from the bed. By backtracking, we saw that someone had been following the buck's tracks but had turned back just 75 to 100 yards short. That deer's tracks were distinctive in the snow because it was dragging a leg.

If you're unable to follow up on a wounded deer because of job or other obligations, try to find someone else who might be able to.

Author with trophy nontypical buck bagged in Saskatchewan with a Knight muzzleloader during late October.

Richard P. Smith is an award winning outdoor writer and photographer living in Marquette, Michigan with his wife and business partner Lucy. He is a nationally recognized writer, photographer and speaker who has written 14 books and hundreds of magazine articles.

Smith's last book, Stand Hunting For Whitetails, was published during the spring of 1996 and contains all you want to know about that aspect of deer hunting. His other books include Great Michigan Deer Tales, Understanding Michigan Black Bear, Deer Hunting, Hunting Trophy Black Bear, Hunting Rabbits and Hares and Animal Tracks and Signs of North America.

Smith writes a Regional Report about Upper Peninsula happenings for Michigan Out-of-Doors Magazine and contributes to Michigan Sportsman and Woods-N-Water News. His writing and photography are used regularly in national magazines including Outdoor Life, American Hunter, Bowhunter, Petersen's Hunting, North American Hunter and North American Whitetail.

The author is a recognized expert on deer and black bear behavior and biology as well as hunting these species of big game. He has hunted deer and bear extensively in Michigan and throughout North America for more than 30 years.

Index

157

Books by Richard P. Smith

STAND HUNTING FOR WHITETAILS - Learn how to use the most popular and productive whitetail hunting method most effectively. Discover the best places to hunt from stands, when stand hunting can be most productive, how to avoid being detected by deer when hunting from the ground and elevated stands, how to stay warm during cold weather, how high to go in tree stands and how to reduce the chances of falling. Boone and Crockett bucks taken from stands are covered, including the new Wisconsin state record bow kill. You will also join baseball stars Wade Boggs and Jimmy Key with the New York Yankees on a successful trophy buck hunt from stands. (256 pages) **Price: $18.50 postpaid.**

TRACKING WOUNDED DEER - Nobody likes to wound a deer, but it sometimes happens. This is the book that will help prepare you for the time when you have to follow a deer you've shot and will increase your chances of recovering wounded animals regardless of where they are hit. Must reading for bowhunters since trailing arrowed deer is part of every successful hunt. **Price: $19.50 postpaid.**

GREAT MICHIGAN DEER TALES - If you like reading about BIG BUCKS, you will want to read this book. It contains more solid information about Michigan's most memorable bucks than any book previously published. If you are interested in bagging a BOOK BUCK , studying this collection of success stories will help make it happen. There's no better way to learn than from those who have already accomplished the feat. **Price: $15.50 postpaid.**

DEER HUNTING (2ND EDITION) - This best selling book was so popular it was updated to include even more information and photographs. The second edition includes 260 pages and 139 photos that show and tell you all you need to know to successfully hunt whitetails and mule deer throughout North America with modern firearms, muzzleloaders, bow and arrow, and camera. Bonus chapters on deer biology and management, hunting ethics and more. There's something in this book for you whether you are a beginner or an experienced veteran like the author. **Price: $18 postpaid.**

UNDERSTANDING MICHIGAN BLACK BEAR - This book was written for the person who wants to learn more about black bears; their habits, life history and behavior in addition to how to avoid problems from them when in bear country. One of the chapters is a history of bear attacks. The text also provides valuable insights into bear research and management in the state and efforts that are currently underway to ban bear hunting. **Price: $16.50 postpaid.**

HUNTING TROPHY BLACK BEAR - A 328-page hard cover volume with 157 photos. Information on this book's fact-filled pages tells the reader all about hunting this controversial big game animal, covering all of the bases as far as hunting techniques, guns and bows. Record book bears, hiring a guide, bear biology, management and the future for black bear and more are also covered in the text. **Price: $23 postpaid.**

HUNTING RABBITS & HARES - A 153-page soft cover book containing 130 photos. The first complete book written on the subject that tells all there is to know about hunting all species of North American rabbits and hares with shotgun, rifle, handgun, black powder arms and archery equipment. Additional chapters cover population cycles, tularemia and detailed photos show how to butcher these small game animals without cutting the body cavity open. **PRICE: $10 postpaid.**

ANIMAL TRACKS AND SIGNS OF NORTH AMERICA - This book has 271 pages and lots of photos. It's the first guide book including actual photos of wildlife tracks and sign rather than sketches. Bonus chapters cover aging tracks, tracking wildlife and much more. **Price: $18 postpaid.**

**Send orders and
make checks payable to:**

Smith Publications
814 Clark St.
Marquette, MI 49855